HEY, MOM

Positive Approach to Parenting

SYLVIA SPICER

Las Vegas, Nevada

HEY, MOM

Cover Art: Sheryl Spicer
Cover Design: Michael Purcell
Layout and Editing: Fay Klein
Layout Consultant: Kate Hawley

Library of Congress Cataloging-in-Publication Data
Spicer, Sylvia, 1954-
  Hey, Mom / Sylvia Spicer.
        p.   cm.
ISBN 1-884724-11-6 (Hardcover/Library Binding).
ISBN 1-884724-10-8 (Softcover trade)
  1. Mothers and sons. 2. Parent and child. 3. Parent and teenager. 4. Love, Maternal.   I. Title
HQ755.85.S68   1999
306.874'3--dc21   98-46697
                                         CIP

Published by Women of Diversity Productions, Inc.
5790 N. Park St.
Las Vegas NV 89129
Phone: 702-341-9807
Fax: 702-341-9828
E-mail: dvrsty@aol.com

Preface

I often think about my childhood days: fading rays of sunlight after supper, the sound of children playing hide and seek on their way home through the neighborhood, searching for every last bit of joy in the day as the street lights beckoned them home. I recall shivering beside the bathtub while my Mother hurriedly toweled me dry in a race with the bath water swirling its way down the drain. I remember exploring drawers full of mystery and intrigue, and learning wisdom from the lining of my father's pocket. Those memories fill my mind now whenever I face a struggle. They are part of the mortar that has held me together through the years. They are my inheritance: a peaceful and secure joy, an inner harmony, a love deeper than emotion.

From the time I started baby-sitting in 6th grade and saw "The Sound of Music" the first of 72 times, I knew that someday I wanted children of my own. I wanted them to be as happy as I had been in my childhood and to be able to savor fun and meaningful memories.

I enjoyed taking classes simply for the pleasure of learning something new, so I was disappointed that for the most important task of my life, being a parent, there was no formal training. I enrolled in education classes and studied child psychology, adolescent development, and abnormal psychology. I read parenting magazines and everything Piaget and Dr. Spock had to say on the subject of raising children. I listened to my experienced friends regarding the highs and lows of their child rearing experiences. In the end, a few weeks before my son was born fifteen years ago, I decided to disregard the theories of all the experts. I couldn't effectively practice their techniques, which seemed to me to be insufficient, unreliable, and unsatisfactory. I decided to raise my child from familiar material, from experiences in my own childhood that made me feel loved, and without any preconceived notions or expectations other than what was good. Our foundation from the very start was that good is ever-present and no matter what the human situation seemed to be, the solution would be found in what was good and right about it. Our choice in life would be to be happy and to look for the blessing in each situation. Whenever a decision was required, we would try to make one consistent with and developed from this base.

Looking at my child through transparent lenses and treating him as an equally sensitive and valuable human being soon became my way of life. As I taught him the principles of life, he taught me some of life's marvelous possibilities. No longer did I merely see the world through his eyes; I was re-learning the early lessons of my life and began experiencing my adult world with child-like innocence. I was now in a dual role as the teacher and the student and this perspective made all the difference.

This book contains excerpts from our life together. They are recorded here for Zach, as an expression of my gratitude to him for teaching me how to live a constructive life by showing me the world through the eyes of a child again.

The aftersmile in this book is for you.

Dedication

To my parents, Harold and Hilda Spicer, who put the stardust in my eyes; and to my son, Zachary, who hangs the moon!

Acknowledgements

The author acknowledges that the concepts and ideas presented in this book are not unique to her. An individual's philosophy is drawn from numerous sources throughout life and it is impractical in such a work to attribute concepts to any specific origin. The author is grateful to the wealth of contributors in her background who influenced this philosophy and enabled her to apply and explain it to her son as a way of life.

Train up a child in the way he should go:
and when he is old, he will not depart from it.
Proverbs 22:6

Table of Contents

Part One
The Pre-School Years   1
Chapter 1- Building Foundations   2
Chapter 2- Sheryl and the Rainbow   11
Chapter 3- Bedtime Ramblings   15
Chapter 4- Adjusting to being a
            Single Mother   19

Part Two
The Elementary Years   29
Chapter 5- The Back Seat
            Commentary   30
Chapter 6- Help in the Kitchen   32
Chapter 7- Music Lessons   36
Chapter 8- Sunday Mornings   39
Chapter 9- Motor Mouth Days   45

Part Three
The Intermediate Years   55
Chapter 10- Supportive Humor   56
Chapter 11- Tinted Windows   63
Chapter 12- Hometown Lessons   66

Chapter 13- It's Your Dream   69
Chapter 14- Just Jesting   72
Chapter 15- Pass the Peas   76
Chapter 16- Twice Times Good   82
Chapter 17- Puzzle Me a World   86
Chapter 18- Plastic Petunias   90
Chapter 19- Wake Up   93
Chapter 20- Best Friends   96
Chapter 21- Just Wondering   100

Part Four

The Teenage Years   105
Chapter 22- Country Living   106
Chapter 23- Media, Sex, Bikes &
            Regrets   110
Chapter 24- A Great Day for Ducks
            and Polar Bears   119
Chapter 25- Tournament Time   125
Chapter 26- Poster Girls   128
Chapter 27- Government Begins
            at Home   130
Chapter 28- Breaking Up   133
Chapter 29- Tides and Bulldozers   136
Chapter 30- Ego is Your Goliath   140

Chapter 31- Step Ahead   144
Chapter 32- Education is
            Appreciation   147
Chapter 33- Mealtime Humor   151
Chapter 34- Save the Garden
            and the Song   153
Chapter 35- Vice Money   156
Chapter 36- Right Relationships   159
Chapter 37- Measuring Up   165
Chapter 38- Advancing Years   170
Chapter 39- Remember When   177
Chapter 40- What is a Parent   181

Epilogue   183

PART ONE

The Pre-School Years

When Zach was born, friends warned me that there would be sleepless nights, labored days, and very little time for my own pleasures. It wasn't so.

When Zach was two, friends advised me to buy running shoes for playing chase and sedatives for us both to take when he started shouting "No" in response to my requests. It wasn't so.

When Zach was four, friends claimed that I should prepare for more than I could handle, that he would start demanding his own way. It wasn't so.

1
Building Foundations

Hey, Mom, it's time to get up!"
"What time is it," I yawned.
"The little hand's on five and the big one just went past the six."

"It's too early."

"How early is it?" Zach questioned.

"So early that the moon hasn't given up the night yet. Go back to sleep, please."

∞

At an early age I learned from my parents that joy is a constant awareness of an aftersmile and that it is present in every situation. After successfully enduring each life experience there often seems to be a moment when a person pauses, takes a deep breath, and with a broad smile and a twinkle in the eye, is able to exhale a statement of relief, "I made it." For two years I had been confused by my divorce and had forgotten the relevance and effect of an aftersmile: the calming reassurance of an unconditional love. Now, as a single parent and without financial assistance from my ex-husband or government agencies, I was about to have the significance of an aftersmile reestablished for me in radically new terms. The following pages examine the role of this aftersmile in our lives.

∞

My neighbor, a delightful woman retired from teaching kindergarten, immediately adopted Zach and me when we moved next door to her. She provided a patient, loving ear and her husband was very kind to offer me the use of his tools for home improvement projects for which I wasn't equipped.

One day as we sat gliding in her porch swing, I attempted to explain to her my approach to Zach's learning situations. She kindly reminded me that Zach was only a year old and most likely did not understand the concepts I was trying to teach.

I gave her comment a great deal of thought for the next several days. He was only one and didn't have much of a vocabulary. I wasn't sure what change I could make other than to suspend my explanations to him altogether.

Zach admired pretty objects and when he would approach me carrying a Waterford crystal candy dish, we would examine its beauty together, discuss how it intrigued him, and then I would locate one of his toys and offer him a trade. "Deal, Zach? Let's make a trade, OK?" He would consider the trade and then relinquish the fragile article without objection. In this way I could rescue the antique and not anger him to the point of crying or causing a disturbance.

A few weeks later I was again relaxing in the glider with my neighbor. In my hands I was fumbling a toy that Zach had earlier deposited with her. From his position in the grass, Zach eyed the toy, and then, during a pause in the conversation, he quietly offered me a handful of freshly picked dandelions and suggested, "Deal, Momma, pwetty yewo woses?" After this incident I felt confident that we had communicated effectively.

∞

"Hey, Mom, can you play with me?" I raised my eyes from the computer screen and refocused on Zach. He had dressed himself that day in his favorite red plaid shirt. The shirt tail on his right side hung two inches lower than the left as a result of his putting the first button in the wrong hole. His blonde head was covered with a blue Twins baseball cap worn slightly askew and the left leg of his green sweat pants was bunched together at the knee from the overlapping knee sock. Zach owned several nicely coordinated outfits , but he never wanted to get them dirty so they hung neatly in his closet every day.

I hated to turn down an offer for a good time, but my deadline was quickly approaching. "I can't play right now, Zach. I'm preparing some documents for work."

Every few minutes his sweet voice repeated the request. Unlike Zach, who demonstrated the glory of childhood by managing to concentrate on playing a game of memory while watching TV and listening to my requests, I tended to focus so intensely on the project at hand that I was unable to accomplish more than one task at a time.

"Zach," I pleaded, "if you don't stop bothering me, I'm going to lose my temper. Please give me a few quiet moments to finish my work and then I will be happy to play with you."

Zach waited for a few more minutes and

then inquired, "Have you found your temper yet, Mom?"

What an interesting observation, I thought. What is a temper anyway and why is it so frequently and easily lost? Is the old temper worth finding or should a more pleasant disposition be permanently substituted?

Zach's comment reminded me of James Stewart's line in the movie *Harvey*. Elwood P. Dowd had been advised by his mother that in order to succeed in this world one had to be "ever so clever or pleasant." Elwood stated that he "had been clever and would now recommend pleasant." With this reminder, I reprioritized my duties and interrupted my attempt to be clever at work in order to play pleasantly with Zach.

∞

I know that I looked forward to holidays as a child, but I don't recall having the same degree of anticipation and enthusiasm that Zach had. To him, every day was a special day and holidays were even more so. He began decorating the house and celebrating Thanksgiving the day after Halloween and continued beating WalMart and other retailers to the holiday punch throughout the year for each successive occasion.

∞

"Hey, Mom, why hasn't Santa left anything in my stocking yet?"

Christmas was still a week away, but Zach was standing on tip toes squeezing his empty stocking that was dangling by a single thread from the mantelpiece. The glow from the fire illumined his eager blue eyes. I could see the disappointment in his face when he found the stocking empty and I wanted to soothe him. "He probably won't stop by our house until closer to Christmas, Zach, because he has to deliver gifts to lots of homes."

Zach pondered my response and then with raised eyebrows proclaimed, "He shouldn't have many deliveries to make this year, Mom, because I haven't seen that many good boys."

∞

I was fortunate that Zach loved to be around people from a very early age. He enjoyed playing with children and adults and managed to mingle at the appropriate age levels. It eased my mind to know that he looked forward to time at day-care every morning as I hurriedly unloaded him and rushed off to work. The afternoon sessions weren't quite so much fun for him because the only time Zach ever consented to take a nap was when he was not feeling well and nap-time was mandatory in the afternoons at day-care. But Zach used his diplomatic skills and convinced the day-care women that he could be very good at playing quietly in a room by himself while the other children were sleeping.

∞

"Hey, Mom, today at day-care I got into trouble."

I gave Zach a surprised look. His previous reports on daycare activities had always been very positive and Zach was not the type of child who was inclined toward trouble. "What happened that got you into trouble?" I questioned.

"Well," Zach hesitated with his hands positioned securely on his little hips, "I was playing on the floor with Charles. I had 30 blocks and he had 50 blocks. He decided he wanted to play with more blocks so he started to take mine. When I told him he couldn't have them because he already had enough, the teacher got mad at me for not sharing with him and put me in the corner."

His depiction of the event made me want to chuckle, but the frankness of his voice and his wrinkled brow warned me against any such display of pleasure at this moment. So I responded sympathetically. "That's too bad, Zach. What did you learn from that experience?"

"Never trust a man who has more blocks than you!"

∞

"Hey, Mom, what can we do on such a cloudy day?"

I looked across the room at puppy Tup. She had been romping all over the house completely unaffected by the gloomy weather outside and was currently being entertained by a piece of fluff on the floor. "Let's think like a puppy! " I encouraged.

Zach cocked his head to one side and studied the simple pleasures of being a pup. He had just sprawled out on the floor next to me to play with the pup when the telephone rang. Zach jumped up and raced into the adjacent room to answer it. "Wait just a minute, Grandma, while I go get my Mom. She's in the living room thinking like a puppy."

2

Sheryl and the Rainbow

When Zach was nearly four, my 38 year old sister passed away. Sheryl had long been my inspiration. I am glad that I was able to be with her at her passing, but letting her go was the most difficult task I had ever experienced. The lesson of Sheryl and the Rainbow that I learned from Zach was a comfort to me then and also seven years later when I said good bye to my mother for the last time.

"Hey, Mom, why are you and Grandma crying?" Zach was attempting to ease gently into a delicate issue.

"We're sad because your Aunt Sheryl passed away and we won't see her or be able to share good times with her anymore." Zach had spent the week with us at Sheryl's house and had displayed a great deal of sensitivity to his Aunt and the strenuous, heart-breaking situation. I knew this had to be difficult for a four year old to understand.

Zach gently stroked my face with the back of his tiny hand, wiping away the tears. "Are you sad when there's no rainbow in the sky, Mom?"

I wondered what that had to do with how sad I felt right then, but more than once before Zach had switched from being a care-free child to having an adult understanding of a situation and I was willing to learn from his innocent wisdom. "No," I responded hesitantly.

"Well, Mom, you told me once that even though I could only see a few colors and half the shape of a rainbow, it was really a full circle of lots of colors." I recalled an earlier discussion with Zach about Noah's Ark and the significance of the rainbow in that story. I had told him that a rainbow is a reminder that God is keeping His promise.

"Remember, Mom?" Zach persisted. "You said the beautiful blessing of a rainbow is always with us even though we can only see it on certain rainy days."

"That's right." I affirmed. "There's always a potential for a rainbow because there's always a blessing at hand."

Zach continued his lesson with certainty

and clarity of purpose. "You know what I think, Mom? I think somewhere there is a rainbow in the sky. I think right now God is smiling quietly and helping Sheryl on the other side of that rainbow. She is still happy and safe. You said the beauty of a rainbow and the happy way it makes us feel can always be with us. Then Aunt Sheryl can always be with us too, in our thinking. So maybe we should just think of each day as a rainbow day, Mom, and keep Sheryl in our thoughts."

Tears rolled down my face, but this time they were in gratitude. Zach was emulating the meaning of his name, God's gracious gift. I held his fearless face gently between my hands and kissed the bridge of his nose and whispered, "Thanks for the lesson, dear, and for being so sensitive and wise."

Zach's explanation that day brought me instant relief and rainbows continue to play a significant role in reminding me to be grateful instead of mournful when I think of deceased loved ones. Only my regrets died that day because Sheryl was still very much a part of my life. Not only did I have wonderful memories of our past experiences together, but the good and beautiful traits which constituted her life continue to affect me now. Her life was part of the circle of my life. I began seeing situations from her refreshing perspective and sense of humor and felt the assurance of her continued love.

∞

After Sheryl passed away, her youngest daughter, Keirstin, visited us on occasion.

"Hey, Mom, is 6 1/2 years old older or younger than 6 years old?"

Keirstin had been shadowing Zach all afternoon and the two of them had found several subjects to debate. Anticipating a debate on age, I replied, "6 1/2 is older than 6 and you are 6 3/4 which is older than 6 1/2."

Zach turned to Keirstin, puffed out his square chest, and proudly stated, "Hey, Keirstin, guess what? I'm older than you, I'm six and three pennies!"

"Not three pennies," I laughed, "three quarters!"

3

Bedtime Ramblings

recall my parents reporting to their friends that they were amazed at how willing I was to go to bed when I was young. I never had to be told twice and often volunteered on my own. This wasn't extraordinary to me because bedtime was so much fun. My mother would tuck me in, wipe the hair from my forehead, and place a kiss in the clearing she had created. My father would arrive shortly and sit on the edge of my bed and read stories to me from my collection of A. A. Milne and Robert Louis Stevenson. He had a marvelous reading voice and his training in Children's Literature provided me with a wealth that not every child was as fortunate to experience.

These one-on-one times that I cherished so much with my parents I passed on to my son. We would routinely read stories, chat about his seemingly endless curiosities, and then , if we both hadn't already fallen off to sleep, I would quietly strum country tunes and Broadway hits on my guitar. Zach knew when it was time for lights out because, at his request, we ended the routine every evening with the song, *Over the Rainbow.* He mentioned once that his favorite line from that song was, "the dreams that you dare to dream really do come true." I asked him why that line in the song meant so much to him and he responded, "Well, Mom, dreaming is like hoping, and hoping is trusting that promises are being kept, like trusting in the rainbow to be there when you need it."

∞

"Hey, Mom, I'm tired. Will you lie down with me until I fall asleep?"

"Sure, Binker" (my pet name for Zach). As I pulled back the bed-covers to let Zach crawl in, I noticed a lump under his pillow. "Hey, Zach, what's this box of coins doing under your pillow?" I inquired.

Zach crawled under the covers, laced his fingers behind his head, smiled very assuredly, and explained, "Well, Mom, there are so many kids losing teeth at my day-care, that I thought the Tooth Fairy might need a loan."

∞

"Hey, Mom, when you were pregnant with me what did you want to have, a boy or a girl?"

Was this a trick question, I wondered? I didn't want to offend either gender, but I did remember my preference. "I always wanted a boy, Zach. Girls are nice too, but if I could only have one child, I wanted it to be a boy."

Approving of my answer, Zach added, "Yeah, Mom, and if you can only have two, two boys are nice to have also.

∞

Most nights after I tucked Zach in bed, I would gather his dirty clothes from a pile on the floor and empty the contents of his pockets onto a table in order to avoid subjecting the washer and dryer to the hazards of his pocket collection. One evening his pants weighed in heavier than usual so I made note of the contents of the four small pockets and considered Zach's purpose for salvaging each item. His treasures could not be discarded because each item performed a unique and necessary function.

There was one shiny rock for kicking

around, a rabbit's foot for tickling his face, two walnuts kept in reserve as a snack for his favorite squirrel, several gum wrappers folded into zig zags for a neck chain, snail shells for the fish aquarium, a pine cone for fragrance, a smooth piece of glass used as a substitute worry stone, and a large bird feather used for stirring up a breeze on a warm sultry summer's day.

His treasures reminded me of the difficulty I had dusting my own bedroom shelves which were appointed with crumbling clay sculptures from daycare, crayola sketches of our travels, and love letters of apology and appreciation from Zach. He had obviously inherited this collecting trait from me so I smiled as I added his pocket collection to the table containing the smooth rocks, shells, and driftwood which I had acquired on a walk that day.

4
Adjusting To Being A
Single Mom

As a single parent, I was fortunate to have a support group close at hand. My folks lived on the north side of town and we lived on the south side, a distance of less than five miles, far enough for separate lives and yet close enough to meet emergency needs.

In Zach's first year, I was relieved to learn that my parents were only seven minutes away when I sent out a plea for help at 4:00 a.m. after Zach had been crying without pause for several hours. I didn't know what to do. This child depended on me, alone, to make the correct decisions regarding his well-being and happiness. I tried everything I knew to calm him. He didn't have a fever, rash, or any other physical symptom which would have led me to call a doctor. He was not teething and his ears were okay. His diaper was clean, his belly was full, and nothing appeared to be sticking him anywhere. What was the problem? He couldn't talk to me in words and I didn't understand this strange crying. I drew him close to my chest and sang to him, but he didn't respond in the usual manner. Not knowing what to do terrified me and I felt very alone and helpless. I needed some advice and reassurance.

My parents arrived with their overcoats covering their pajamas and my father gently took Zach from my tired arms. Within two minutes Zach was sleeping peacefully on Dad's shoulder. I was, of course, greatly relieved that he was no longer suffering, but I was also a bit perplexed. I walked into the adjacent room with my mother and asked her what had been wrong with Zach. She smiled and said, "Nothing was wrong with Zach, dear, what needed changing was you." I was surprised by her answer, but continued listening to her explanation of how Zach had sensed my fear and impatience and was responding to it by crying. I knew she was probably correct in her assessment. I had had a stressful and longer than usual day at work and had not resolved the thoughts troubling me before coming home. Since I had returned home late that evening, I had hurried through supper time, bath time, and story time with Zach. I was so exhausted by eleven p.m. when I finally started putting him to bed that I was fighting back my own tears. Zach responded to my fast heartbeat and troubled expressions the only way he knew how - by crying for me. My frustration had triggered his tears and my fear from not knowing why he was crying perpetuated them.

Twelve years later our family was vacationing with my brother when he encountered a similar situation with his first child. Steve was in much need of rest when his year old daughter began crying and his efforts to calm her were to no avail. Once again my father gathered the child into his arms and she calmed down. Steve shook his head in amazement and I reiterated my mother's words to him, "There's nothing wrong with the child, what needs changing is you."

∞

My hometown was a wonderful place to live as a child; however, living here as a single parent has been challenging. After spending four years in an out-of-state college, three years in Graduate School at a Big Ten University, and two years of single life in Texas, this small community which offered a protected environment for my child seemed to offer me very little activity.

When my husband left our marriage, he returned to his former lifestyle. He was free to socialize, pump iron, exercise, ride his bike, play ball, go to the movies, sail, fish, hunt or whatever he desired just as he had done before we were married with no concern for anyone else. For a while his freedom bothered me since I didn't seem to have the same privileges anymore, but soon I realized that as a parent of a newborn, I too could do all of these things with some adjustments. I socialized with Ernie and Bert and the Sesame Street gang every morning and afternoon. I pumped iron with one hand along the length of the iron-ing board as part of my daily laundry rou-tine. I rode my bike as far as I could peddle it with Zach strapped in the child seat behind me and a saddle bag packed full of diapers, powder, lotion, wipes, a change of clothes, toys, juice and water bottles, gra-ham crackers, cheerios, peeled grapes, a teething ring, and sunscreen. I played ball with Zach by rolling a racquetball along the floor toward his outstretched legs and hoped he would pick it up before the dog retrieved it and changed the game to "keep away". I went to every Disney flick suitable for an infant and sailed on distant voyages with Zach in the evenings during his bath time. I fished for substance in pureed food, and hunted through toy boxes for pieces to complete a child's puzzle.

One situation where I had difficulty adapting was the "don't fit" area. I was a single parent and all of my friends were either single without children or married. I didn't fit either category. My single friends didn't want to have children around and my married friends didn't want a single woman around their husbands. I tried to solve this dilemma by finding a suitable mate for myself, but that, too, was difficult. I had loved my husband and waited until his third proposal before deciding that my "forever" would be with him. I knew we had differences that needed compromising, but I was certain that my love for him would endure. I felt hurt, betrayed and abused by the man

I loved. These strong feelings didn't make dating someone else very easy so for the first two years I chose not to date. Besides, there didn't seem to be any time for it. I had a full time job which required that I bring work home in the evening. By the time I finished my homework, housework, and spent some time with Zach, I was too tired to be civil to myself, let alone to anyone else.

One day, in Zach's third year, he brought home a nice man for me. As I sat on the porch watching Zach ride his Big Wheel on the sidewalk, I noticed that he stopped to talk to a man walking down the street. The two of them journeyed back to our house together where Zach made the appropriate introductions and invited the man to stay for dinner. He accepted the invitation and assured me that our menu of macaroni with sweet pickles and cheese was one of his favorite meals too. Time revealed that the gentleman would have been a marvelous father for Zach, but not a suitable husband for me. I continued my search for a good husband/father figure through seven more men, but each one could only be categorized singularly, either as a good father or a good husband and I wanted one who could be both. Seven men over a ten year period may not seem like a fair sampling, but I thought it was sufficient for a small town population. Instead of continuing my search for the one man who could be everything to me and with whom I could share my affections, I decided to surround myself with lots of people, male, female, older, younger, single, and married who could offer me a variety of insights and broaden my horizons. I began appreciating all the good a person had to offer and didn't concern myself too much with what appeared to be negative traits. Suddenly the focus of my world broadened and I enjoyed several friendships and developed creative areas in my own personality of which I had previously been unaware. Somehow having several friends and interests seemed to require less time to maintain than did one intimate relationship and so I never resumed my man-hunt.

I had returned to this small town after my divorce because I wanted Zach to have the benefit of knowing his grandparents as I had known mine and my parents had known theirs. My folks were a marvelous source of support which I tried not to abuse and I, in return, made myself available to them to help with house and yard tasks. On one occasion, I responded to a call early Saturday morning to remove a rattlesnake from their basement.

If my parents hadn't lived in this town, I would have moved elsewhere. My training and area of expertise had no outlet here. I was forced either to commute for three hours a day, which would provide me with more money and mental stimulus, but very little time for Zach, or resign myself to a different occupation which was less than exciting for me, but kept me close to home. Several times when boredom at work tempted me to accept employment opportunities elsewhere, I reflected on the quality of life Zach and I had together with our extended family and chose to remain where we were. Money was not a strong motivation as long as we had enough to meet our needs. I had been employed since I was fourteen and in the early years had made it a practice to save half of my earnings. These savings helped to buffer us through some meager years. I believe my decision to choose a job that would allow me to spend more time with Zach rather than one that would provide us with more financial gain was a wise one.

One evening after spending all afternoon shopping in various stores, we were roasting marshmallows in the fireplace when Zach commented, "Hey, Mom, we sure spent a lot of time comparing price tags on everything we did today! Isn't it nice that there's no price tag on times like these by the fire?"

"It sure is." I responded. "Don't ever put a price tag on happiness."

∞

Life has been a constant learning and re-learning of fundamental principles. I was introduced to many of them as a child and have been re-experiencing their truths in various degrees through different life situations. The depressions in my life, my divorce, the loss of loved ones, and loneliness were all opportunities for me to learn more about myself and the existence of an "Eternal Now." I discovered that feelings of anger, remorse, and bitterness were based on a regretted past while feelings of anxiety and fear were based on an unknown future. I couldn't change the past and could only learn more about the present in order to help my future. My feelings here and now could be anything I wanted so I chose to feel happy. This mental practice I used whenever I was tempted to feel otherwise and I taught this principle to Zach at a young age. This is not to say that we never had problems, because we had several, nor was it pretending to be happy without cause or ignoring problems. Our approach was to elevate our thinking from an attitude of "poor troubled me" and focus on the blessings at hand. We expected good results and dismissed the possibility of returning to a previous depressed condition already outgrown. No detailed road map to the future was necessary because what happened along the journey to teach us life's lessons was insignificant. The lessons themselves were the important part. We stopped wondering why loved ones died and no longer worried about what might happen in the future. It was enough to know that our faith in a power greater than our own provided us with everything necessary for a peaceful rest each day.

PART TWO

The Elementary Years

When Zach was six, friends counseled me that his vocabulary and attitude would change now that he had started school. It wasn't so.

When Zach was eight, friends contended that he was too old for me to rock in a chair and was beyond the age of calm discussions. It wasn't so.

5

The Back Seat Commentary

I was fortunate to have my mother as a confidant for many years. We frequently purchased vanilla cokes at the local drive-in diner and then discussed the joys and problems of the day. Zach usually accompanied us on these outings and entertained himself quietly in the back seat. On one occasion, he began reading aloud and interrupted the serious conversation I was trying to have with my mother.

"Hey, Mom, the back seat of a car sure is a good place to do some reading."

"It certainly is, but could you please read quietly to yourself until I finish my conversation with Grandma?

"I am reading to myself, Mom, because nobody else is listening to me."

∞

Zach's attention was suddenly drawn to the persistent crying of a young child in the car next to us. "Hey, Mom, why is that baby in the next car crying so loudly?"

"He's trying to get the attention of his parents."

Zach rolled up his window and shook his head slightly. "Boy, he won't have any trouble when he goes to Kindergarten."

"Why is that?" I questioned.

"Because he sure knows the short vowel sounds!"

∞

"Hey, Mom, I finished my sandwich. Should I leave the container here in the back seat?"

"Yes, that's OK for now. I'll throw it away as soon as I finish my sandwich."

"Mom, don't you know that it isn't polite for you to eat in front of Grandma when she isn't eating?" Zach said.

I recalled teaching him that courtesy earlier in the week but his reminder surprised me since he had also been eating and he knew that rules applied to everyone. "You just ate in front of her!" I reminded.

"No, I didn't, Mom, I ate behind her."

6
Help in the Kitchen

Preparing meals was a family affair. Zach would sit at the kitchen table and talk things over with me while I cooked. I never thought he paid much attention to what I was doing until one day when I was not feeling well and was slow getting out of bed. I heard the floor of my doorway creak just in time to see Zach carrying a tray full of food to me. He had fixed me a spaghetti breakfast complete with garlic toast and orange juice and he had decorated a napkin with the words, "Hop you fel beter soon, Mom" on it.

∞

One Saturday morning Zach was perched on top of the kitchen stool with legs swinging freely and phonetically reading the content labels on the food products I was using in preparation for lunch. Deciphering his pronunciation of most of the eighteen plus letter words was difficult, but one term stumped me completely.

"Hey, Mom, what is a nitwit?" Zach inquired in his typical curious tone.

"Someone who acts silly or misbehaves, why?"

"Because the label on this can says it is nitwit soup."

I put down the carving knife, wiped my hands on my apron, and examined the curious label for myself. That particular day it wouldn't have surprised me if nitwit had been the author of the label instead of an ingredient. Zach pointed to the term in question and I immediately laughed. "That's net weight, Zach, not nitwit."

∞

"Hey, Mom, are all of these leftover cookies from the Christmas party ours?"

"Yes, Zach. They are for us to share."

"Oh, boy," he exclaimed hopping on both feet, "my best dreams have come true! Hey, Mom, if I sold all of these cookies to my friends I'd have some real dough!"

∞

One evening while I was cooking dinner with Zach's assistance, I inquired what items and quantities he thought were contained in certain recipes. His version of stone soup and chili intrigued me especially since his quantities were in diminishing order as was typical of Zach's pattern of speaking. For such a progressively thinking child, it intrigued me that he spoke in regressing order.

<u>Stone Soup</u>

Cut up about 30 to 20 carrots, 15 to 14 potatoes, 12 to 10 green beans, and pour in a can of red stuff. Add one teaspoon of water and cook it for about 3 hours until it bubbles.

<u>Chili</u>

Pour in a can of red stuff, add three or two noodles, and a hand full of gooey, smashed hamburger. Cut up 6 to 5 onions and cook for about a minute.

Of course, my favorite recipe was one for Elephant Stew which a friend suggested that I send to my brother. I sent a note suggesting that if I didn't hear from him soon, I would attempt to locate the ingredients for Elephant Stew and bring it as a covered dish to the Thanksgiving dinner at his In-laws house. His wife called me within a few days of receiving the note and recipe and suggested that I bring a salad.

Elephant Stew

One elephant (medium size) salted
Two rabbits (optional)
Brown gravy to cover
Cut the elephant into bite size pieces. Add brown gravy and cook 18 hours at 465 degrees. This will serve 3800 people. If more are expected, two rabbits may be added, but do this only if necessary as most people do not like hare in their soup.

7
Music Lessons

ach played the piano whenever I was available to encourage him to practice. As a preschooler his light touch and delicate control of melodies was no threat to the instrument and was a relief from the ear-piercing banging that some children engage in when left alone at a piano. He expressed his emotions through the keys so that it was easy to detect what he was feeling when he played. When he was eight, he began lessons which he took for three years, and made steady progress until his enthusiasm waned under the disciplined regimen. He mastered his recital piece, but seldom played for enjoyment anymore. Then, too, there was the conflict of other activities that made heavy inroads on his time — homework, paper route, and athletics. I miss hearing him play and seeing the joy in his eyes when he completes a difficult piece. I think someday he may regret it too.

One day his assignment was to identify notes on sheet music. He tried to escape the lesson by leaving his music at Grandma's house, so I gave him some of my sheet music to work on.

"Hey, Mom, what note is this in your piano music?"

I identified the note as a B. "You've read that note in your sheet music. Don't you remember?"

"Sure, Mom, but these are adult notes in your music so I thought they might be different."

∞

One evening Zach shared a valuable insight on life as he finished practicing the piano. "Hey, Mom, what song do you want me to play for you now?"

I had had a difficult day so I requested that he play something cheerful.

"Mom, are you sad?"

"I'm a little upset over something that happened at work today. My boss asked for my opinion and when I expressed disagreement with her views, she was unhappy with me."

"Well," said Zach after a moment's reflection, "I guess life is like playing the piano, Mom."

"In what way, Zach?"

"You told me once that when playing the piano, it's just as important to play the rests as it is to play the notes. In life, maybe what you don't say is just as important as what you do say."

8
Sunday Mornings

Early Sunday mornings were reserved for "life lessons." During this time, I would read to Zach from the Bible and he in turn would ask questions about what I read. We then discussed how the lesson could be applied in our daily lives. His questions were challenging and generally quite thought provoking. Some concepts were difficult to explain to a child so young, but Zach let me know if I had communicated an idea successfully by adding his own insight to it.

∞

"Hey, Mom, remember in the 23rd Psalm where it talks about the shadow of death? Why does the writer use the word 'shadow' there?"

I studied Zach sharing the fireplace hearth with two cats and a dog, each one slightly overlapping the other in an attempt to get closer to the warmth of the fire. His sturdy back sloped gradually toward me as he hugged a pillow and patiently waited for my response.

"Perhaps the author used the word shadow because he didn't believe the process of dying changes a person anymore than walking through a shadow changes a person." I reminded him of the walks we took at night and how the street lights caused shadows to be cast on the ground by the big trees. We walked right through those shadows, from the light into the dark shadow and back into the light again without changing. "Death doesn't change us either, Zach. It is just a moment of doubt, but the fear and doubt go away just like the darkness disappears when we walk back into the light."

I paused to see if he was understanding this concept. Once before we had talked about darkness being the absence of light. I had explained that the only place where darkness exists is where the light is obscured or there is nothing present to reflect the light, as in outer space.

Zach was observing the rays of sunlight from the window prism that were dancing on the floor. "So does that mean that light is more powerful than darkness?" he questioned.

I searched my mind for something in his

past that he could relate to in this situation. "Yes, Zach, light is more powerful because it destroys darkness. When you were two, you told me that you liked your bedroom because, with the street light outside your window, nothing could ever 'put the dark' on you. You were right about that, nothing ever can."

Zach rolled over and smiled at me and said, "I think I understand, Mom. The shadow of death is like walking past a tree at night and walking through its shadow. Nothing happens when you walk through a shadow...unless," he paused with a mischievous look in his eyes, "you happen to walk through the shadow of a falling tree."

∞

"Hey, Mom, why did the high school boy commit suicide if death doesn't change anything?"

"I guess he never understood the significance of shadows." I knew there were many situations that made people feel hopeless: bleak prospects for success in the future, loss of family and friends, feeling the need for an unknown change, thinking there was nothing to do to improve a situation, or not being able to bear up under past mistakes. When these feelings of insecurity appeared, it was time to come back home! "Home is safe, Zach, it's base; it's where one is confident, and good is visible; but it is not a geographical location, it's a mental sense of security." Zach was studying me very carefully. "It is the ability to see the good hidden in a pile of doubt. It is our hope for the future.

Zach began stroking the black cat who had won pole position in front of the fire. "What about when I do something wrong, Mom?"

I assured him, "When you misbehave, I'm not pleased with your actions, but I continue to love the great amount of good that is always present in you. That is the unconditional part of our love for each other."

"Uncon.... what did you say?"

"Unconditional. That means no matter what mistakes we might make, we can always be confident in knowing that no wrong deed can ever separate us from the love we receive automatically based on our natural goodness. There is always good present, so we are always loved.

"Have you ever felt really depressed, Mom?"

"Yes, I was in a very dispirited mood one day after my mother passed away. I didn't feel well and I was worrying about my miserable job and my limited finances. I didn't see much hope that the circumstances would improve in the future. I took a deep breath, cleared my thoughts, and observed the blessings at hand. After I opened my mind to more positive thoughts a feeling of relief came over me and I wrote down the ideas in the form of a song for you to remember if someday you find yourself questioning your future prospects."

Aftersmile

One day my life seemed so bleak and dreary
And my prospects for success seemed few;
I just sat with head in hand and wondered,
When these thoughts from Truth came shining
    through:
When you're looking for a dream, come Home;
When you need someone to care, come Home;
When you're tired or you're scared
Or you can't think what to do,
Raise your head, look for Me,
come back Home.

When you feel the need to make a change,
Or you think there's nothing left to do,
Look around, there is hope,
    See My aftersmile in you.
Raise your head, look for Me,
come back Home.

You don't need to go away,
Your perfect rainbow's here this day.
Raise your head, here I Am,
welcome Home.

9
Motor-Mouth Days

ach loved elementary school and was very fond of the teachers who relished an occasional laugh with him. Typically he pounced through the door like Tigger and stampeded me with his smile as he related a story about the day's events.

∞

"Hey, Mom, I got all A's on my report card this period!"

Zach's return home from school was a daily welcome sight. He beamed with excitement and delighted me with his buoyant optimism. "That's great, Zach, but can you explain why the teacher added a comment on your card about your talking too much in class?" Suddenly I realized that my comment might de-bounce my little "Tigger," but before I could rephrase the question, Zach offered an explanation.

"Well, Mom, it's like this. There are so many kids that come to school unhappy and depressed that I try to cheer them up and make them laugh after I finish my own work. I guess the teacher doesn't appreci-

45

ate my humor."

I was relieved that my comment hadn't altered his focus. "I don't think its your humor she doesn't appreciate, it's probably your timing. Why don't you save your humor for recess and lunch time. Kids need to be happy then, too."

∞

Looking through family photo albums was a preferred pastime of Zach's. He would approach me with his arms bulging full of albums and plead, "Let's do some remembering, Mom!" I seldom declined the opportunity to reminisce, so we leaned toward each other on the sofa and Zach stretched his arm around my broad shoulders and wove my long brown hair between his fingers. We identified the people and places in the photos and then Zach started us off on "remember whens" and other comparisons.

"Hey, Mom, look at this picture of you when you were little. It's black and white just like the pictures on *Donna Reed, I Love Lucy* and *Mr. Ed.* Was the world all black and white when you were a kid?"

"No, Zach, the world was colorful then too, but the cameras just didn't show it."

"Hey, Mom, did you ever make mistakes when you were little?"

"I sure did, lots of them, and I still do." I hoped that he wouldn't request that I itemize all of them.

"You always try to think everything through so carefully that I didn't think you would ever make a mistake."

"Mistakes aren't bad, Zach. They are stepping stones to correct actions and reminders of what we shouldn't do." I considered some of the stressful situations I had encountered in life and how I had used them as indicators of my progress. "For every problem there is a solution, but the answer is not found in the problem because the problem and the solution come from different sources. Once you've uncovered a problem, you need to change your mental station. Stop focusing on the problem and tune in to the answer channel. By not making that same mistake again, you can measure your progress. If you really learn the necessary lesson the first time, you won't repeat the mistake."

"What kind of mistakes have you made, Mom?"

Several of my mistakes instantly came to mind. "Most of my mistakes have something to do with my lack of patience. I must have been born in the fast lane because I find it very difficult to be patient with myself and others when progress does not occur as rapidly as I think it should."

At first, Zach seemed surprised to learn of my mistakes, but soon he flashed me a look of relief and asked, "How does a person learn patience, Mom?"

I delayed for a moment to consider my response. Patience was still very foreign to me but I was making some headway. "A person can learn patience by observing nature. Sometimes I try to learn patience by watching a duck learn how to fly or by examining a rose." I recited to him a poem about a woman who was impatient with nature's timing and decided she would help the petals of her garden rose unfold since all of her other flowers were in full bloom. As a result, she forced open the delicate petals which very quickly withered away. "Beauty is revealed in its own time and in its own way. Our plans need to include enough patience to see our ideas through to fruition. A good idea requires our patient, unhurried support."

∞

"Hey, Mom," Zach called from the tire swing "when you were little, did you ever play games and compete with your friends?"

I watched him spinning quickly as he unwound in the twisted-rope tire swing. "I spent most of my childhood playing outside with the neighborhood kids. Why?"

After a brief shake of his head to regain equilibrium he started twisting clockwise in his swing again. "I just wondered who won the games when you played, Mom?"

"I always did," I muttered without hesitation.

Zach stopped his wind up and gave me a puzzled look. "Were you that much better than everyone else?" he questioned.

"Heavens no," I laughed, "but I always thought I had the most fun. To me, the person who had the most fun was the winner of the game. You are the best expression of your blend of qualities" I explained. Zach raised his feet releasing his hold on the earth and began spinning again. "Nobody else can be you. For that reason, you shouldn't wish that you were as talented as someone else, because that individual has a different blend of qualities. In competitions, you will always win, regardless of the score, if you decide at the outset that you are going to try to have the most fun." Zach had come to a halt in his swing and spied the log spanning the riverbed which he sometimes used as a balance beam. I paused to see if our conversation still held his interest and then continued to explain that the purpose of sports is to have fun. If people don't enjoy the activity, they are defeating its purpose and are not adhering to the spirit of the game. I reminded him that in the games of ancient Greece, the winner of the race was the runner who crossed the finish line first with his torch still aflame. To be the fastest runner meant nothing if the athlete finished with a flameless torch.

Zach had successfully balanced his way across the log and was now kicking a discarded paper cup that had blown into the yard. After a few small dribbling dodges, he gave a swift kick and sent it soaring across the turf. "Mom," he commented, "I understand the rules in the old days about keeping the torch burning, but we don't play with torches now."

I gazed at his smiling face and said, "Your smile is your torch. Keep your smile intact whenever you play a game and you'll always cross the line as a winner."

∞

"Hey, Mom, can we talk about something?"

"You bet! Why don't you sit down here and help me pot some plants while we talk."

"OK, Mom." Zach had a look of frustration about him and was fidgeting with his pocket collection. "I don't know what to do about some friends of mine who don't seem to like me anymore."

"What makes you think they don't like you?"

"They say things that hurt my feelings and they poke fun at my new friends."

I was curious to know how much thought Zach had given the problem so I asked, "What have you thought about doing in this situation?"

Zach reflected for a moment and replied, "I thought maybe I should just ignore them and play with my other friends."

"Oh," I said warily, "so you're thinking about throwing them away? Look at your hands, Zach. See how dirty they are from potting plants? Do you plan to throw your hands away too?"

Zach was shocked by the suggestion and retorted, "No! They're the only ones I have. They'll be fine after I wash them."

"Friends are precious too, Zach," I said with a nod in his direction "and sometimes hard to find."

He contemplated the correlation I had made and suggested, "So you think I should have a talk with my friends and see if I can wash away some of the dirt?"

"That sounds like a good start. The so-called 'dirt' that you see on your friends is no part of them, really, anymore than the dirt on your hands is part of you. You don't have to destroy your hands; you just need to wash them." Zach finished packing the soil around the plant in his pot and brushed the dirt from his hands.

"I think I'll start cleaning things up now." he said as he headed out the door. I watched as he made his way through the wooded lot toward his friend's house and I felt confident he would be successful.

PART THREE

The Intermediate Years

When Zach was ten, friends argued that I should consider enrolling him in a military school before he became hard to handle. It wasn't so.

10
Supportive Humor

ne evening upon my return home from work, Zach greeted me with, "Hey, Mom, you won't believe what kind of day I had at school."

I shed my coat and gloves, put down an arm full of papers and asked what had happened.

"The teacher made me sit in the back of the room all by myself."

Misbehavior at school was not common with Zach who enjoyed the challenge of trying to please everybody, so in bewilderment I inquired what he had done to warrant that punishment. He was standing in front of me tugging at his shirt-tail and rolling it up and down his arm as though his arm were a sticky rolling pin.

"The teacher gave us a pop quiz in U. S. geography today and I was wearing my Santa Fe Trail T-shirt with all of the western states on it" he said pointing to each state with his free arm. "He made me sit behind everyone else during the quiz." Then, with a chuckle to himself, he continued. "After the test, I asked the teacher if he would please check with me before he gives a quiz the next time so I'll know what to wear."

∞

Zach seldom failed to offer a supportive comment whenever it was needed and he was very quick to find the humor in absurd situations. Indeed, from an early age he displayed a remarkably mature sense of humor.

∞

"Hey, Mom, you like to sing, play the guitar, shoot hoops, build things, and work on cars. Isn't there anything that makes you afraid?"

"Just one thing, Zach. Sometimes I'm afraid of not being loved."

Zach rose from his chair where he'd been doing his homework and gave me a big hug and kiss. "Ah, Mom, you solved that problem a long time ago when you had me. I'll always love you, unconditionally, remember? You said nothing could ever separate us from an unconditional love." With the thumb and index finger on each hand he made two circles and locked them together. "We're like this, Mom, forever!" he said showing me his hands. I looked at the design he had made and thought about the term forever. His two connected circles resembled a Moebius band, the symbol for infinity. I knew he was correct in what he had said because the interesting fact about a Moebius curve is that the inside of the curve becomes the outside in one continuous motion. If we were part of that curve, then we could never be separated.

I gave him an extended hug and kissed my favorite spot on the bridge of his nose. "You're exactly right, Zach. Thanks for the reminder."

∞

"Hey, Mom, what are you doing now?" Zach queried from his thinking spot on the staircase.

"I'm paying bills and balancing my checkbook."

A few minutes elapsed and again he inquired, "Why do you have your eyes closed now, Mom?"

I opened my eyes and looked up at him. The sun coming through the stair landing window backlighted him so that only his outline and golden hair were illuminated.

"I'm just giving thanks for coming out in the black instead of in the red."

"What does that mean, Mom?"

"It means that we had enough money to pay all of the bills."

"Maybe next month you can be thankful for coming out in the green instead of in the black!"

"What do you mean by that, Zach?"

"If you're in the green, you're in the money, and that's better than coming out in the black."

"I sure like looking at life through your eyes, Zach."

"Yeah, sometimes life's funnier that way, and it's usually more colorful. I like rainbow days, don't you, Mom?"

"Every day with you is a rainbow day for me, Zach."

∞

Carom, known as Flip to Zach, provided enjoyable entertainment in the evenings. We would place the board on the floor, lie pronated supported by our elbows, and flip the painted wooden rings until our middle finger got too sore to continue any longer. "Hey, Mom, where are we going for spring break this year?" (Flip went another of Zach's rings into the corner pocket.)

"Oh, I thought we might go back down to the Florida Keys. Would you like to go deep sea fishing while we're down there this time?" (I aimed and shot for a side pocket, but missed.)

"Gee, that would be great fun. Where could we rent a submarine for catching all of those deep sea fish, Mom?" (I flipped again as he commented and this time my ring ricochetted off the piano.) The mental picture I had of using a submarine to catch fish deep down in the sea started me laughing.

∞

"Hey, Mom, I just heard on the store radio that a child was injured in a car accident. What would you do if that happened to me?"

"I would be beside myself!"

"Really, Mom! You mean if I were the one injured you'd be beside yourself instead of beside me?"

"Hey, Mom, listen to this description

about being a guy. It mentions some funny situations."

Zach began reading aloud to me from a book of syndicated humor that he had been enjoying while I was selecting meat and eggs. I chuckled at the first few depictions of life as a guy and then stopped. After a few pages Zach asked me why I was no longer laughing.

"I find the jokes to be offensive and rude, Zach."

"But, Mom, the author is only kidding." He retorted.

I knew the author meant to be funny, but he was doing it at the expense of others and I didn't care for that type of humor.

"Think about the types of situations which you find funny, Zach. You find humor in paradox and you report it in such a way that even the most pristine ears can enjoy it. Your humor doesn't need censoring and yet it brings laughter."

Zach realized that I was serious about this concern and asked, "Does that mean you would rather I not read this type of material, Mom?"

I didn't want to appear to be over protective but I did want him to diversify his reading material.

"I think it is sad there aren't more role models today engaging in clean humor because laughter is very important in life. Perhaps you should read the humor of other authors to learn how they handle and view similar situations." I named a few authors and Zach agreed to read their works. A few days later he raised the issue again.

"Hey, Mom, I read the books you suggested and I understand now what you mean. A comedian never knows who the audience is going to be so I guess it's better not to offend anybody so that everybody can laugh together."

11
Tinted Windows

As I entered the family room with an arm load of clean laundry, I saw Zach looking out the window while raising and lowering his sunglasses on his nose.

"Hey, Mom, do people with blue eyes see the world differently from those who have brown or green eyes?"

I could usually tell when Zach was about to pop a question, but I never knew what the question or my answer would be.

"I don't think so, Zach. It isn't the shade of our eyes that colors our world, it's our biases and prejudices." I placed the basket on the sofa and began folding the clean shirts.

"Is bias what makes some people want to hurt me even when I'm nice to them?"

"It could be." I suggested. "Those people who try to hurt you are people who possibly don't like themselves, or are afraid, or don't like people who are different from themselves and they are taking out their anger on you. They may not be aware of all the good around them because they've allowed their self-image and their image of others to become clouded." I reminded him of the story from my childhood about a vacant house with tinted windows where children liked to play. Each window in the house contained glass that had been tinted a different color. The children ran to separate windows to view the world beyond their windowpane. The first child saw a red world, the second saw everything in blue, the third saw only green, and the fourth saw only a yellow world beyond the pane. Finally they all arrived at the clear windowpane, without any tint added to the glass and saw before them a world full of different colors creating a beautiful scene.

"What lesson can we learn from this story, Zach?"

Zach had raised one side of his glasses so that his left eye looked through the tinted lens and the right eye viewed the world clearly. "We can learn that things aren't always what they appear to be and sometimes our own biases determine what we see."

"That's right. Your friends may be seeing

themselves and others through windows that are distorted by their own prejudices, biases, and self-will. They may need someone to lead them to the clear glass window where they can view themselves and others without any distortions."

"How can I help them find the nice part of themselves and others so they will stop hurting me?"

I looked at his "cool shades" and suggested, "I think the method will become clear to you when the time is right, but until then, you might start by removing your own colored glasses."

12
Hometown Lessons

ur town is a quaint Hoosier town safe for raising children. It is a clean community and, for the most part, a progressive one. But there were times when buildings were demolished and vacant lots left in great abundance. These vacant eye-sores provided an opportunity for a lesson.

∞

"Hey, Mom, why do people tear down nice looking buildings just so they can leave an empty lot for weeds to grow in? It doesn't make any sense. I could understand it if they were going to build another building there, but some of these lots have been vacant for years."

I agreed that they weren't pretty, but I knew there could be many reasons why they were left vacant. "Perhaps they were the result of a fire, an unresolved zoning issue, or perhaps there was a lack of funding and plans had to be changed." I suggested that in some instances, people are too quick to condemn and criticize. "Criticism should be constructive, not destructive. These vacant lots are reminders to us not to criticize someone else's ideas unless we have some better replacement ideas. If we don't pro-vide constructive criticism, then all we leave after condemning an idea is an ugly void, similar to the vacant lots around town, a place for weeds and animosity to grow. Before you remove what is already intact, make sure you have something desirable to replace it."

∞

"Hey, Mom, do you want me to help with your flower garden?"

I welcomed the help. "That would be great! Would you please pull the weeds while I set out new plants?"

"I guess I could do that, but I'm not sure that I know all of the different kinds of weeds so I might miss some."

I didn't have the energy or the time at that moment to instruct him in botany so I asked if he knew which plants were flowers.

"Sure" he replied "they're the pretty ones that smell good."

"Then that's all you need to know" I assured him. "You don't have to be able to identify all of the weeds if you can distinguish which ones are flowers. As long as you can identify the good things around you, you don't need to be able to understand and itemize the bad."

"Is that why you don't want me to say bad things about people?"

I hadn't considered that correlation before, but I agreed that he was correct. As long as he was focusing his attention on the things that bothered him, he was obscuring the good qualities. "Zach, the solution to a problem is found in what's right about it. You don't need to be able to diagnose and analyze everything that's wrong. Just uncover the problem and handle it."

Zach loosened the soil around a weed with his trowel, gave the stem a yank, replaced the dirt, and patted it firmly. "I think I understand" he sighed. "If I don't search for the solution, I'll get buried with the problem."

13
It's Your Dream

Hey, Mom, I'm sorry about getting in trouble yesterday. I guess I didn't make a very good decision." Zach had been so concerned that his friend would think he was weird, that he followed his friend's advice even though he knew it was probably wrong. "Mom, after I made the mistake, I just hoped that nobody would find out how stupid I had been. I've been having bad dreams about it ever since. What should I do?"

"One reason that it is so important to tell the truth is so you can sleep peacefully at night." Zach was a sensitive person and couldn't lie to his conscience. "Deep down inside, the best part of you knows the truth about the situation. Your good judgement reminds you that you didn't heed better advice. But there's no reason for you to continue to have sleepless nights once you've learned your lesson and have decided never to make that same mistake again. Sit down here and let me tell you a story."

I began with "once upon a time" and told

him the story of a little boy who had misbehaved during the day and had been sent to bed early. While he was asleep, he had a dream. With lots of suspense and expression I continued...

The little boy dreamt that he saw a monster outside his bedroom window. It was a fierce looking monster, more graphic than any Spielberg movie character. Its appearance was extremely frightening and its behavior paralyzing.

The little boy was so terrified by what he saw that he darted across the room to his bed and dove under the covers. Cautiously, his head emerged from the pile of comforters as he heard the ominous footsteps approaching. By now, the monster had entered the hallway outside the little boy's room and was peering in through the open door. The little boy was horrified and jerked the covers clear up to his chin, clenching them in his tiny fists.

But the monster brazenly continued toward the bed. With this, the little boy drew the covers up to his nose, but the monster still advanced closer and closer. By this time, the little boy was so distraught that he could hardly breathe. But the monster kept coming closer, and closer, and closer until he was right beside the little boy's bed glaring down at him. The little boy did not know what to do. He was shaking the bed-covers in fright and with trembling lips he stammered, 'whaaaat are youuuu gggoing to do nnnow, monster?' And the monster scowled at him, started to roar at him, but suddenly stopped and then in a baffled voice responded, 'I don't know, it's your dream.'

Zach gave a sigh of relief. He had forgotten that it was just a dream and the only power that the monster had was the power that the little boy gave him. "Your thoughts govern your experiences, Zach. If you keep your conscience clear during the day, there will be nothing to frighten you at night."

With a wink and a smile Zach went off to bed.

14
Just Jesting

Hey, Mom, we're studying Japanese customs and U.S. price comparisons in school. Did you know that in Japan one pound of hamburger costs $7.00?"

"Holy cow, Zach, I couldn't afford to feed you if we had to pay Japanese prices!"

"They must be holy cows, Mom, if they cost that much!"

∞

"Hey, Mom, this internet is great fun. Thanks for subscribing to it for me."

"I'm glad you are enjoying it, but I asked you thirty minutes ago to please take the trash out to the curb and you haven't done it yet."

"I'm sorry, Mom, my mind must have been on screen saver."

∞

"Hey, Mom, why do you keep after me to pick up my dirty clothes and keep my room clean?"

"I keep reminding you because you never seem to do it unless you are reminded several times. It's not a difficult task if you do a little every day."

"Gosh, Mom, I can't be perfect. Would you rather have me keep a clean room and choose to smoke, drink, and use drugs?"

"Definitely not! I guess that's my cue to ease up a bit on cleanliness, huh?"

"That's OK, Mom, I'll try harder."

∞

"Hey, Mom, today's a week-end. If I invite the guys over will you play basketball with us?"

"Sure, but why do you need me to play if the guys are going to be here?"

"Because TJ won't come over unless he can play on your team and Moose is still trying to find a way to defend your turn-around-jump-shot."

∞

"Hey, Mom, how about sitting down with me and watching some TV before we leave for basketball? We still have 45 minutes before practice starts."

"Okay" I said as I plopped down on the sofa next to him, "but I sure could use something to drink."

"Would you like me to draw you a map to the kitchen, Mom?"

"Hey, Mom, look at that cat over there by the new jail. What is it doing?"

"It looks as though it's hunting for its dinner."

"Maybe it's looking for jailbirds, Mom!"

∞

As I pulled up next to the gas pump at the filling station Zach hustled out of the car and began filling the tank. Usually he meticulously washed each window as the tank filled, but on this July afternoon he slumped back down in the car seat and waited for the pump to shut off.

"Man," he exclaimed, wiping sweat from his brow and the back of his neck, "you know it's hot outside when the temperature is higher than the price of gas!"

∞

A person's size has little correlation to one's age. Zach was very long when he was born and exceeded the height chart as a young child. His tall stature amazed so many people that when he was three, I presented his birth certificate at Disney World in order to receive a child's discounted ticket.

I was accustomed to Zach's height and the

awkwardness that sometimes accompanied it, but he surprised me one day at Hardees when I saw his 5'10" body shaking vigorously.

"What are you doing?" I asked.

He stopped vibrating the room and picked up his container of orange juice from the table. "The label on here says to shake well before opening!"

15

Pass the Peas

"Hey, Mom," Zach questioned as he shuffled the playing cards for the next round of Crazy Eights, "what was the most important lesson you learned from your Mom?"

I watched as he dealt the cards and I organized my hand which was very red and void of eights. "I think I would have to say it was the lesson I learned about passing the peas." His grandmother was a very gracious woman and sensitive to the needs of other people, but she had developed a curious way of asking for something at the table. "Remember how she would say, 'Would you care for some peas?' when the peas were already located in front of the person addressed?"

"I remember that. Why would she ask for things in that manner, Mom?" Zach turned over the first card and the game started with spades.

"Because whether or not the person wanted peas, the individual would be almost constrained out of courtesy to offer her the peas. In that way, her need was satisfied without her directly asking for what she wanted." I reflected on her indirect technique of asking for something and realized that there was much more to it than simple finesse.

"Her action of offering the peas," I continued, "embraced several qualities and attitudes toward life which she was teaching me. It practiced the Golden Rule by offering to others what she would most like to receive. It symbolized trust that there would be an ample supply of peas, and it expressed her sensitivity to the needs of others. It also affirmed her trust that others would have love and consideration for her needs by returning the offer of peas."

I could see from his confused expression that he didn't understand how not asking for peas could do all of that, so I explained that he'd probably understand better as he observed a variety of personalities. "Sometimes, Zach, individuals are so self-absorbed in what they want or need that they fail to sense the needs of others. They might say, 'no thank you' to more peas and never consider their role in ministering to the needs of others by passing them the peas. Their mind may be so strongly focused on the obvious issue that they don't hear the heart's message."

"I see, Mom. They forget to pass the peas to others even though they don't want any for themselves."

"That's right."

"But, Mom, what if they don't pass the peas back?"

His Grandmother's lesson addressed that issue too. "If we show steadfast faith and refuse to fear a lack of good, then we will recognize and accept the good already available."

Zach was still not satisfied with my explanation and fanned his cards repeatedly. "What if you offer the peas to an enemy who takes all of them?" he asked.

"That's certainly a possibility" I acknowledged and drew another card, "but then your offer shows a trust that love is returned in kind. If you show loving concern for the needs of others, eventually they will reciprocate. It is difficult to be an enemy to someone whose every action expresses love and concern for you." This was a concept I wanted Zach to understand so I pursued the lesson. "Passing the peas exemplifies selflessness, compassion, trust and gratitude. All of these are necessary traits for living a happy life. It's tempting to believe that changing your mood from being sad to being happy takes time, and that there is a necessary recovery period." I explained that if his team lost a basketball game, he didn't have to wait until the following week to see the good things his team did accomplish during the game. Or if he had an argument with a friend, he didn't have to wait for a certain length of time before he made amends. "It doesn't take time to forgive, to forget, or to feel happy again. Time is a human concept used to estimate when relief can be expected. In reality this moment is the appropriate time to express happiness and gratitude for the blessings already at hand. This," I emphasized, "is the moment when we are grateful for the peas that have been passed."

"Won't people feel you are manipulating them by acting this way?" he persisted, changing the suit to clubs.

I looked at my red hand and drew again. I didn't think being sensitive and courteous to others was a form of manipulation. "It is no more manipulating than when a seeing-eye dog warns a vision-impaired master of an approaching danger. The dog observes the danger, communicates the warning, and offers guidance by suggesting an alternate path, but the master must still decide whether to accept the dog's keen sensitivity and follow its lead."

Finally I drew an eight and rescued my over-sized hand. "Remember, Zach, it is the love that satisfies people, not the person doing the loving." This was an important difference and I wanted him to understand this concept so he wouldn't be quick to feel "used" when he helped someone and they later appeared to reject him.

Zach repeated my statement as though he were shuffling it in his thoughts prior to accepting it.

"Passing the peas," I summarized, "demonstrates loving others as you love yourself. It also demonstrates compassion for others and enables you to rejoice in the bounty of good available to all without being envious."

"Gosh, Mom" Zach grinned as he played his last card "I'll be remembering an awful lot the next time I pass the peas."

16
Twice Times Good

Late one evening, just as I sat down after cleaning up the dinner dishes, Zach informed me that he had a science project due the following morning. Four hours later while I was reshelving the creative supplies and picking up paper triangles from the floor he gave me a big hug and asked, "Hey, Mom, how can I ever repay you for all of the things you've done for me?"

A long list of ways to help my tired body accomplish the remaining house chores came to mind, but I decided to settle on two points. "You repay me twice, Zach. First when you are grateful for what you have received, and second when you pass on the good things to your children or to someone else."

Zach was a bit relieved, I think, to discover that I was being philosophical instead of practical and decided to encourage me.

"How did you know how to raise me all by yourself, Mom?"

That was an easy one to answer. I knew

how to love him because my parents had first loved me. "Grandma has passed away now, Zach, but you continue to receive her blessings from the good qualities she taught me that I pass on to you. So, when I'm loving you, I'm loving her too and repaying her loving-kindness to me."

Zach began asking me particulars about being a single parent and reminded me that it had been difficult at times. "A person can choose to view life as a problem or as a joy." I instructed. "When your father left, I was three months pregnant and had no job. He closed our joint bank accounts, sold our home, abandoned the idea of being a father, and left me on my own. I was looking up hill at what appeared to be a difficult future." I had envisioned two people loving and supporting each other as they raised a child and sharing the responsibilities, concerns, and joys. I was devastated to learn that not only did I not have someone to love and support me, but I had to count on my own stamina and judgement in performing a difficult and important task: raising a happy, healthy child. "I could very easily have become discouraged by suddenly assuming the burden of being a single parent - being the bread winner, the comforter, the playmate, and the disciplinarian all at the same time. Instead, I chose to view it not as a burden, but as a joy."

"But, Mom, that was a lot of work for just one person."

"It certainly was, Zach, but whenever I was tempted to feel too tired to entertain you, or to listen to your quizzical motor-mouth, or to read just one more story before bedtime and rock you to sleep, I thought about how tired my parents must have been every night; yet they never failed to make memories with me that would carry me through my childhood and through the difficult times in my life. So, I played dominoes, memory, and crazy eights with you when I was too tired to think; I listened to your little rhymes having heard the same ones daily for several months; I crawled around the battlefield of our living room floor in search of matchbox cars, and the piece of bubble gum you lost earlier in the day; I consented to watch Winnie the Pooh for the umpteenth time even though my favorite movie conflicted with its time slot; I delayed my quiet time an extra hour when at bedtime you requested not to go to bed just yet so we could listen to the night sounds."

"It sounds like you're due for a rest!"

"Yes, but because I chose to do all of those things I could view them as a joy instead of as a burden. You can choose the way you view situations too. You decide whether you will be happy or sad. By making all of these choices to spend time with you, I was expressing love for you and repaying my mother's kindness by honoring her memory. In that way, I was loving her too."

"Gosh, Mom, in order to be a good parent do you always have to sacrifice yourself?"

"No, Zach, I didn't lose anything; I gained everything. That wasn't self-sacrifice, that was love."

17
Puzzle Me A World

As a single parent, I sometimes found myself attempting to be a super-mom in addition to being a hardworking employee, faithful friend, devoted daughter, concerned sister, and accommodating neighbor. Some days, not even the bathroom provided a haven from hassles. Almost as soon as I shut the door, I would hear the scratching of a cat wanting safe entry, a barking dog wanting to continue his chase of the cat, children needing immediate answers to questions they had forgotten, and of course, phone solicitors. But just when my schedule seemed ready to explode, Zach would remind me that children have hectic times too.

"Hey, Mom, I don't think I'm going to survive this week. It's the end of the semester and I have semester exams. On top of that, I have my piano piece to practice before Sunday's recital, a basketball tournament this Saturday, and my paper route to deliver every day. Do you have any suggestions?"

That seemed like a very busy lineup to accomplish in such a short period of time,but I was certain Zach had the necessary tools to accomplish the task set before him. "You have to put each situation into a practical and proper perspective. Don't let the situation dictate your actions through fear. Disarm the fear first and then the solution will have a better chance of being revealed to you." I told him a story about a father who was frantically attempting to churn out his doctoral dissertation when he suddenly found himself the lone supervisor of his energetic and precocious six year old daughter. His plan was to organize a variety of games to keep her busy all afternoon while he worked at his computer.

The father parceled out the games one at a time. When the little girl finished the first game, she collected the pieces, carried them to her father and asked, "What can I do now, Daddy?"

He issued a second game and continued with his work. Half a page later, the daughter returned, repeating the request, "What can I do now, Daddy?" These frequent interruptions continued through three more games until the father realized that he needed to find a more challenging task for his daughter. The next time she returned, he gave her a picture puzzle of the world and told her to go into the adjacent room and put it together. When she was finished, (much, much later he hoped) he would find another task for her.

He had almost completed the next page of his dissertation when he was interrupted again by her soft plea, "What can I do now, Daddy?" He was appalled! "Why didn't you finish the puzzle?' he questioned. "But I did, Daddy!" she replied. "You couldn't have finished it in such a short time. There's no way you could have put the entire puzzle of the world together correctly." With a pleading voice the little girl said, "But I did, Daddy, come see." The father walked briskly into the adjoining room and stopped suddenly and examined the completed puzzle on the floor. He was amazed! How in the world had she managed to assemble that puzzle so quickly and accurately? He didn't even know many adults who could have done it so quickly. He looked down at his daughter and she said, "It was easy,

Daddy. On the back of the puzzle was a picture of a man, and when I put the man
together, the world took care of itself!"

Zach gave a chuckle and said, "I've got the
picture. When my life seems hectic and out
of control, I need to stop worrying about
how to get everything done and just put
first things first in order of importance."

"That's right, Zach. Relax, find the joy in
what you're doing, and puzzle me a world."

18
Plastic Petunias

Whenever Zach and I deliberated a serious matter, I made every effort to teach him how to think about a general problem and not what to think. In this way, I hoped that the carry-over value would be broad reaching and not limited to a particular time, place, event, person, or situation.

"Hey, Mom, how do you know if something is real or true?" Zach explained that he and his friends had different opinions on some of the ideas discussed at school and he wasn't sure which opinion was correct.

"If something is real or true, it is pragmatic." I answered. "You can demonstrate its principle and prove its truth."

"What do you mean by that, Mom?"

I needed an example and I noticed his math book on the table. "Think about the laws of mathematics. Two plus two equals four, and you can demonstrate that fact by adding two apples to two oranges and counting the total number of fruit to arrive at the sum of four. But if you believed that the sum of the two numbers equalled five, you could not prove that statement."

I remembered a story from my childhood about a woman who loved flowers so I modified it to illustrate a point to Zach.

A woman lived in a small apartment and filled her window box with an assortment of pansies and petunias. She enjoyed caring for the flowers as part of her daily routine and they in turn flourished under her loving care. One winter, a friend of hers could not find any real flowers to send on a special occasion, so the friend sent her a potted plastic petunia which retained its color with no care required. The woman continued to care for this plastic petunia the same way in which she cared for all of her real flowers. Each day she would greet it cheerfully and carefully check the color of its leaves and the dampness of the soil to be certain it was receiving enough water and sunlight. However, no matter how much attention she gave it, it still never changed from being a plastic petunia.

I explained futility and the significance of this story to Zach.

"No matter how much you believe in a false concept, Zach, it never makes it real or true. Truth can be demonstrated and is always true. Its principles don't change over time or as they are viewed by different people. Spend your time and energy selectively nourishing what can be proved and be careful not to get side-tracked nurturing a plastic petunia."

19
Wake Up

"Hey, Mom," Zach panted as he rolled to a halt at the porch and sat down to remove his rollerblades. "Pete told the kids at school some lies about JT and I don't know how to convince my friends that what he said isn't true." Zach was concerned that as long as his friends believed Pete, they wouldn't have anything to do with JT, because they had made fun of him when he tried to sit with them at lunch time.

I put down the newspaper and felt fortunate to have completed an entire column on the front page. "What are your options?" I queried.

Without hesitation Zach replied, "I could call Pete a liar and explain to my friends what really happened, or I could tell them a lie about Pete and see how he likes it."

I didn't respond immediately in hopes that my silence would give Zach a chance to think about what he had said.

"I guess those aren't good solutions after all."

"Why is that?" I asked.

Zach placed his foot on my lap and I tugged at his reluctant rollerblade. "Because they are focusing on Pete's mistake" he grunted as he twisted his foot out of the boot, "and you told me once to concentrate on what is right in a situation. I don't want to do anything to hurt Pete's feelings, but this really bothers me."

I knew the situation upset him because he was a peace-maker and didn't like anyone's feelings to be hurt. "Do you remember the story about the little boy who dreamt he saw a monster in his room?" I asked.

Zach recalled the story and summarized it for me. "How does that story apply to this situation, Mom?"

"The monster wasn't real," I reminded, "it was only a dream. No action the little boy took in the dream made any difference or made it a real experience. All he had to do was to wake up and then he stopped per-spiring from his imagined fear."

"Are you saying that lies are like dreams?"

"Yes, they are very similar. The story that Pete told your friends is no more true than the monster was real in the little boy's dream. Wake up and see that you don't have to respond to something that doesn't matter. People thinking a lie about you or anyone else doesn't make it true. Your attempt to respond to a lie gives it authority it doesn't deserve."

Zach shook his head and asked, "How do I get my friends to understand this?"

"Support them in seeing the good in JT instead of trying to point out the lie in the story. Act with kindness toward them; don't react with hostility to the lie." I gave a few detailed examples that illustrated how the only way to defuse a lie was by living the truth, not by arguing to prove its truth. "Preserve truth's integrity through your quiet confidence in it and don't argue against a point that has no merit."

Zach gave his rollers a big spin and handed me the paper. "Life isn't easy," he commented, "but it's a lot of fun. Anything interesting in the paper today?"

20
Best Friends

No one ever thought Zach was short of playmates as he grew up. Repeatedly, while I was talking on the phone, my friends could hear background conversations of children in my house yelling, "Car 54, where are you?" or verses of "a horse is a horse of course of course" being sung.

Entertaining large groups of children at my home was enjoyable since convincing them to obey my wishes was simple once their fantasy character was determined. This bit of child psychology I learned from my mother after watching her walk my younger brother home at gunpoint. Numerous attempts on the part of my father and others had failed to bring Steve home for supper. He was much too busy having fun playing the roles of Superman, Spiderman, and the Lone Ranger to be bothered with eating. So, after a full day of teaching first graders and cooking a five course meal, my mother marched outside in her apron, located Steve in the neighbor's yard, identified his character as a cowboy, drew his own toy gun on him and said, very firmly, "march, partner!" as he reached for the sky. All of this was, of course, very entertaining to the neighbors who had been making friendly wagers on the situation.

Because Zach never seemed to be without a few friendly faces around him, I was surprised when he contemplated the number of his friends one day.

"Hey, Mom," Zach began in his typical manner, "I think I may need to work on my popularity. Everyone else seems to have lots of friends to hang around with and I still only have a few good friends."

I was frustrated with the weed whacker I had been using which seemed to need a major overhaul before each string advancement. His comment was a welcomed interruption. "Do the other kids mistreat you?" I sneezed, trying to dislodge from my nose what little grass did get trimmed.

"No, he replied slowly. They don't dislike me, they just don't ask me to hang out with them."

I presented him with my gloved hand and he obligingly pulled off the sweat stained rawhide as I inquired how many people were in the other group. "Oh, about ten or twelve guys." he informed me.

That number seemed pretty high to me and I wished I knew their secret for maintaining that many people as best friends. "To be a good friend" I explained "requires a great deal of time and effort. I feel fortunate to be able to maintain three or four close friends. I have several other casual friends, but I don't socialize with them very much." I had found that if I got involved in a large circle of friends, I tended to lose my individuality and the ability to reason and make decisions for myself. It was often the consensus of the group that ruled. "Sometimes a group is organized like a dictatorship. For the sake of speed and convenience, sometimes one individual is allowed to decide all issues."

"So more isn't necessarily better." Zach responded.

"That's my opinion." I answered. "Unless they enjoy gardening in which case more help may be better." I gave his neck a pat and returned my long hair to its rubberband. "Zach," I said, "if you believe that you have a few good friends whom you can trust and on whom you can depend to stand with you when you need support, then consider yourself fortunate instead of deficient."

"I guess you're right, Mom. Do you need help with your glove?"

"Not this time," I said as I slid my hand into position, "but I sure could use some help with the weeds!"

21
Just Wondering

ey, Mom, do you know what doubts, fears, and mushrooms have in common?"

"One teaspoon of vanilla, 2 cups of flour..." I was thinking out loud trying to concentrate on the ingredients I still needed to add to my cookie batter. "No," I responded without much thought, "what do they have in common?"

"They all thrive in dark places." He answered. I suddenly took notice of what he had asked, but before I could comment further, he fired another question. "What is permeability?" he asked as I cracked an egg into the bowl and removed pieces of eggshell from the batter.

"Substances flow to an area of least resistance." I instructed. "If an object is considered highly permeable, then it is not very resistant to change. Your skin is permeable because it allows substances to pass through it. Your mind is permeable when it is ready to learn." I looked at the counter where Zach was sitting and didn't see any school books nearby. "Are these homework questions?" I asked.

"Nope, I don't have any homework tonight. I finished it all at school."

"Then why all of these questions?"

"No reason," he replied, "I was just wondering." I returned to the recipe and tried to locate where I had left off.

"Hey, Mom," came another interruption, "why do you think marriages fail?"

I pushed the bowl of half made batter aside and sat down. "Some marriages fail because they don't improve each partner. People tend to limit themselves by placing so much emphasis on sex and passion when their real concerns should be humility and forgiveness." I recalled a simile on sex and language that had helped me better understand the point so I shared it with Zach. "Marriage, based only on sex, is like a language without an idea to communicate. Sex should be the expression of higher affections, people sharing similar interests and goals in life; it should not be a baseless, consuming passion."

"Does it have to be reserved for only one person?"

I had been taught that sex was reserved for marriage, so I began, "Fidelity requires an obligation and it is difficult to be obligated to more than one person. In a marriage each person makes certain promises. These promises don't disappear simply because one person chooses not to keep them anymore."

Zach reached for the bowl and ran his finger along the top edge. He tested the batter and commented that it tasted good but he thought something was still missing. I started to agree when he popped another question. "Why do so many marriages end in divorce these days?"

"People often think thermometrically instead of thermostatically." I replied. Zach gave me a puzzled look so I continued my explanation. "Step over here next to this device on the wall. There are two instruments here, a thermometer and a thermostat. The thermometer doesn't control anything, it only registers the household temperature. It is completely influenced by its environment. The thermostat, on the other hand, controls the household temperature and thereby acts on its environment. You can choose to be affected by your environment, like the thermometer, and acquire all of the same difficulties common to the world today or you can choose to effect a change on your environment, like the thermostat, and make the world the kind of place where you want to live. It's your choice."

Zach reached again for the bowl and I pulled it away. "When will the cookies be done, Mom?"

I handed him the recipe and said, "In thirty minutes if you read me the directions."

PART FOUR

The Teenage Years

When Zach was twelve, friends insisted that the good times were gone and Zach would soon change into a teen-aged brat, unwilling to listen to any kind of advice, and always supposing he "knew it all." It wasn't so.

2 2
Country Living

I understand there is a difference between growing up in the city and growing up in the country. For generations our family tradition at night has been to bundle up the children in the family and take them for "Jammy Rides" after supper to prepare them for bedtime. The country night air is magical. The smell of freshly mown hay coupled with wild honeysuckle, a gentle, refreshing breeze, and the symphony of frogs, crickets, locusts, and owls lull a peaceful soul to sleep. I have always lived near a country setting so I have never missed its charm. My cousin, however, who grew up in the country and then moved to L.A., reminded me of the treasures country living provides. One evening after supper she asked her city husband if they could take their children for a jammy ride in the country. "Country!" he exclaimed, "It would take us two hours of driving to even find the country!"

Dating in rural America resembles city

activities to a certain extent. Teenagers group date and frequent the local pizza parlors after a movie or a few hours at the arcade. They rollerblade all over town and rendezvous at the fountain in the park to wait for parents to shuttle them home. Country teenagers are individuals, but they are fundamentally the same. They are country-born and have country-raised traditions.

Zach and his dates ride their bikes to the same fishing hole I rode mine to with my date when I was a teenager; they walk to the corner, locally-owned grocery store for picnic snacks; they chase fireflies on warm July evenings; they hold their breaths as well as each other's hands while running through covered bridges; they climb the cement footings of arched train tressels and explore the shallow caves of the underground railroad, part of our heritage from the Civil War.

In summer, teenage boys impress their dates at the County Fair, adorning them with prizes. The young adults attend local camps where they experience the power of a sunrise so that they may later appreciate the tranquility of a sunset in the crimson Hoosier skies over fields of corn and soybeans. They search the immense night skies for constellations and find security in the familiar outlines of Greek Gods.

In fall, young beaus and their dates exchange colorful maple leaves, drink cider, and stain their hands gathering black walnuts in competition with the squirrels.

In winter, the paramours race their sleds in the dells and ski across the country landscape echoing the warnings of the beavers who thump their tales on the ice and snow.

In spring, country folk measure their growth on door jams and sip lemonade as they assemble loved ones in preparation for the planting season.

Country life is wonderful. It is important to understand, though, if you plan to pass this way, that as country Hoosiers we measure distance by time and refer to buildings demolished decades ago when offering directions to strangers. We are a hardworking breed with a copious collection of memories. We respect the wisdom of our elders and pay tribute to those who have gone before us by naming schools, athletic fields, and gymnasiums in their memory. In our lock boxes we hold deeds to country landscapes, but in our hearts, both young and old know that the country owns us.

23
Media, Sex, Bikes, and Regrets

n today's media market if a parent doesn't address the issue of sex with a child at an early age, the child may know more than the parent by age six. Not only does a parent have to monitor friends, TV, magazines, posters, 1-900 phone calls, and National Geographic, but now the list is compounded with the addition of home computers on-line to the Internet and visual E-mail. When our household went "on-line," I spent several days warning Zach about revealing too much information to strangers acting friendly on the web and setting boundaries in a world unknown to me, full of child pornographers and abductors. No longer was my child safe sitting at home with me in this era of electronic weirdos. This was a frightening thought.

Zach and I had our first discussion regarding sex when he was five. He had overheard some teenagers talking about how great sex was and misunderstood the terminology they used.

"Hey, Mom," he inquired "what is so great about being six?"

I listed several advantages and then he interrupted, "those are different reasons from the ones the kids down the street talked about."

As he repeated the conversation he had overheard, I realized the topic was "sex," not "six." I explained the subject in terminology appropriate for my grandmother's ear. I emphasized that it was a loving and caressing act shared by two people who had decided to become a family to each other and share all of the joys and responsibilities associated with families. Since that day, the subject has been re-addressed whenever an event at school, an episode in a movie, or a pregnant 13-year old at the grocery store necessitates it.

On one occasion when he was in middle school I likened selecting a partner in sex to purchasing and riding a bike.

"Zach" I said, "sex can be a wonderful act with the right person, in the appropriate situation, and at the right time of your life."

Zach could tell this was going to be a

lengthy simile so he reclined himself in a nearby chair and opened a bag of potato chips.

"It's like choosing a bicycle to buy when you're an adult. When you were three, you were too short and didn't have the strength necessary to balance a bike. If you had tried to ride it at that time you might have gotten hurt or hurt someone else crossing your path.

Zach gave me an understanding nod so I continued.

"Now that you are older and can manage bike riding skills, you are interested in purchasing a bike to use now and as an adult. Even though we live in a throw-away society, we can not afford to buy several bikes so you must choose which style will best suit your needs in the future. You must learn how to care for and maintain your mountain bike on rocky roads and inclines."

Zach dusted the potato chip crumbs off his hands and said, "I understand your point. You're saying all of these traits are also important considerations in choosing a partner for life."

"That's right, Zach. Just because you are

capable of doing something doesn't mean that you should. You need to be able to control your emotions and not let your physical desires control you."

"Mom, do some people have more difficulty than others saying "no" to sex when their body says "yes?"

I was no expert in physiology so I explained that some people simply choose not to control themselves. "If you really love someone, Zach, you will want to do what's right for them and not just what feels good for you at the moment. The feeling only lasts a short time, but the consequences of your actions may last a lifetime if they result in venereal diseases, AIDS, or a child. Just as in the bike scenario, you must be old enough to balance the importance and value of sex in your life. You must be experienced enough in dating a variety of girls to know which one will be a suitable wife. You must be wise enough to maintain the relationship with patience and compassion over life's rocky roads. If you choose the right person, situation, and time, marriage and sex can be a beautiful and rewarding experience for both of you. If your decision or timing is wrong, you could hurt yourself and others."

Zach was tossing the sofa pillow as only a nervous teen-ager can and appeared to have something on his mind. "What's bothering you, Zach?" I inquired.

He began very slowly. "I was thinking about what you said and how you got a divorce. Did you choose the wrong man or did my father leave because he didn't want me?"

The sadness in Zach's voice crushed me and made my heart ache for him. His father had left the marriage when I was three months pregnant with Zach and I hadn't heard from him since Zach was three. "Your father's decision to leave had nothing to do with you because he never knew you. He only visited you twice. His decision made him miss out on a very special kind of joy." I put my arm around Zach and gave him a squeeze. "When I met your father, I had already dated several men and had lived an independent self-supporting life for five years after college. I liked him the moment I saw him and continued to be impressed by his apparent kind nature the more time I spent with him. Unfortunately, because he appeared to be so much better than anyone else I had ever dated, I didn't wait long enough before accepting his proposal. We only knew each other in one setting because we lived three hours apart. Whenever we saw each other we were on our best behavior since our time together was very short on the week-ends. After we were married, we were bombarded with compromises and conditions which we weren't equipped to handle all at once. We had very different approaches to life."

"Was he the wrong man for you, Mom?"

"I don't know if he was the wrong man, but our marriage came at the wrong time. We should have given ourselves more time before we were married to make some of the necessary compromises and adjustments. If we had, the transition to married life might have been easier."

"Do you ever want to see him again, Mom?"

"I'd like to talk to him again someday to tell him I'm sorry for letting my anger take control of me. I was very hurt by his decision to give up so quickly on a wife and young child."

"Did you hate him?"

"No, I loved him, but I didn't know how to keep him happy. He didn't have a very pleasant childhood and in some ways just didn't know how to be happy. He didn't allow happiness to be natural with him the way it is with you."

There was a long pause in our conversation as I tried to hold back tears and squelch the burning sensation in my throat. I knew I still had feelings for his father which might never go away. I needed more time to compose myself so I turned the conversation over to Zach. "Do you feel that you missed out on something by not having a father around?"

Zach positioned the well fluffed pillow behind his head and said, "I don't think so, besides, how could I miss something I never had? Granddad has been a better father to me than anyone I can imagine." He continued the monologue for quite some time describing all of the experiences he had shared with my father. When he finished, I realized that he was correct. He had never known his biological father so there was no memory of him to miss. Since my ex-husband had not contacted us in the past ten years, we weren't involved in custody, visitation, or child support battles. Our situation could have been much worse if we had also had to deal with these issues.

"Do you feel you missed out on something, Mom?"

I knew that I had been fortunate to share so much joy with Zach, but I did have regrets over the divorce. "Yes, but my regret is my own fault. I reacted to your father's criticisms and anger and allowed myself to become defensive beyond my control. I was hurt; so anger was a natural human response, but I should have kept it under control. I gave in to my anger instead of controlling it, so I missed an opportunity to try to reconcile our differences and share our lives together. If I had refused to respond to his fighting, he might have stopped. Since I reacted to him instead of acting positively, I'll never know what good might have been possible."

"Yeah, but he might not have changed and he might have really hurt you someday."

"You're right about that and I would never recommend that anyone remain in an abusive situation. Everyone requires respect; no one deserves verbal, mental or physical abuse. My regret is that I didn't control my initial anger, so I never allowed myself the opportunity to see if a different response might have altered the situation."

Zach stretched his long legs out in front of him and took a deep breath. "Don't worry too much about it, Mom. We've done just fine together. Besides, the lesson you learned from your mistake certainly has gotten the point across to me."

24
A Great Day for Ducks and Polar Bears

Momma said there'd be days like this, there'd be days like this my Momma said..." The radio in the family room played the familiar tune throughout the house. I was the only one home so I cranked up the volume to keep me company as I continued my daily chores. It was a cold winter's day outside and snow had been falling continuously for two days. The schools were not in session due to the blizzard-like conditions and the neighborhood hill was under siege by children armed with sleds, saucers, skis, and slick jumpsuits.

I hummed the radio tune as I poured a cup of hot chocolate to warm me. I had just spent 45 minutes trying to dig out my 50 feet of sidewalk before the snow plow came by again and buried me in slush. It wasn't enough that I removed the snow from the sidewalk, I had to shovel snow that had fallen in the street also. I used to love snow. That white fluffy substance that adorned the neighborhood and ushered in the Christmas spirit. As a child I had spent "snow days" building tunnels and igloos, hauling buckets of snow from the neighbors' yards to complete my fort and snow sculptures. As a young adult I worshipped each flake which enabled my cross-country skis to slide along the terrain. But today I hated the darn stuff. The first few feet that fell were light and fluffy, and no challenge for my shovel, but that had ended at midnight. Now the falling snow was wet and heavy, creating giant boulders as it landed, joining forces with the previous intruders.

I was cold and tired and alone in a mess that I hadn't created. "Why am I killing myself?" I wondered out loud as though someone could hear or might care. I looked around me. The kitchen resembled Pancake Day at Kiwanis. It looked as though an army had eaten in my kitchen. Plates glued together with dried syrup were stacked shoulder high. The remnants of twelve squeezed oranges cluttered the surface of the island work station. A distinct trail of pancake mix could be followed from the counter, past the sink, beyond the toaster, to the stove and all around the gas burner.

Every cabinet door was ajar and the dish sponge was at the bottom of the sink half full of standing water garnished with table scraps and burnt toast crumbs. It was 9:00 a.m. and Zach had taken his friends to the hill in the Dells after feeding them breakfast. I was hungry from shoveling snow, but viewing the mess curbed my appetite. I finished my hot chocolate and decided to rest for a while before tackling the kitchen.

I walked into the family room. "Why in the world do I continue to financially support his pleasures?" I asked myself. The TV was on, but muted and, of course, the remote control was no where in sight. The computer monitor was flashing and the screen saver message read, "Beam me up Scotty" which I would have gladly done if only I had known the correct keystroke. Three blankets were in a heap on the floor under the ceiling fan which was rotating at high speed, chilling the room. The sofa was covered with balls and frisbees of various sizes from the toy box behind it. Zach and his friends had left them there when they couldn't agree on what to play before speeding down the hill on their sleds. This sight was too much to bear and so I wandered into Zach's room.

I was mistaken. Zach's room wasn't a room, it was a dump. Not even the pigs I've known would have agreed to live in it. Posters of The Beatles and the US Women's Gymnastics Team had fallen off the walls and had met each other on the floor. This must have happened recently because they were atop a pile of clothes approximately a foot deep. There were clean clothes mixed with dirty clothes and a sampling of clothing from every child who had ever visited the house. Unmatched shoes of various sizes were heaped in a pile near the closet. Under the bed I found dishes which I bought new but might now be considered antiques. In the closet hung dozens of empty hangers and on the top shelf rested one hat. The dresser drawers were open and the contents draped over the edge. In the dust on a bookshelf was written, "Tom was here." I wished he had dated it. This was too much. Boy, was Zach going to know my wrath when he came home! I couldn't decide whether to ground him for life or to make him endure another lecture. I decided to take a spa while I contemplated my course of action.

Ah, the spa. It's always enjoyable. I pushed back the cover and stepped in. "Ouch! Something sharp scratched me!" I sat down and felt around the floor of the spa for the jagged object. I found it! I had been attacked by a foot long, green, plastic toy shark that Zach and his friends had left behind. As I tossed it out of the spa, I noticed a plastic orca floating upside down. I beached it also and resumed my search for peace. Just as I snuggled into a corner full of bubbling jets, the power went off. The snow storm had turned into an ice storm and the power lines were now down. I wrapped myself in my robe and toweled myself dry as I walked back upstairs. My search for peace had been so tiresome that I decided to resume my chores. Just then Zach bounced into the house with a broad smile on his face and snow clinging to every inch of his bundled body. He removed his outer layer of clothing and I watched as a puddle formed on the floor.

"Hey, Mom, isn't this a great day?"

"Yeah, it's a great day for ducks and polar

bears" I mumbled as I tossed him my towel and walked into my room to try to change my attitude.

25
Tournament Time

March madness in the Hoosier state is a busy period. Basketball for all ages is the topic of discussion at every gathering and dominates the dreams of many children. It was no different with Zachary and our household.

Zach's team had played a game the previous day and had lost. He felt the loss keenly and was trying to justify it in his own mind when he struck up a conversation with me.

"Hey, Mom, I saw the referee talking to you as he ran up the court during our game. Why were you laughing with him when we were losing so badly?"

I felt challenged. I thought he was looking at this incident as one possible explanation for their loss. Zach played on a post season local YMCA team and officials often instructed players and parents while the game was in progress because the sport was considered an educational tool. "It was all in good fun." I mused. "I simply pointed out situations which I thought he had missed, and he educated me on local tournament rules. I wasn't hassling him."

"Yeah, Mom, but the team said the officials made some pretty bad calls that cost us the game."

"They did miss some calls which might have changed game results, but they didn't lose the game for you. Each player on that court made several mistakes. They missed shots and failed to rebound, they committed turnovers, and they lacked proper attention to the game. Unless your team had played perfectly themselves, it's difficult to see how the officials were to blame for the loss."

"I know, Mom, but their bad decisions..."

"What someone else does is beyond your control. You have to concern yourself with what changes you can make to improve your game. But don't lose track of the fun. Athletics is for fun. Winning isn't anything unless it helps you improve all around."

He reflected a while on what I had said. I could see he wanted to defend his teammates and the loss, but he also was fair-minded and he knew they had not played well as a team. "You mean I should keep my torch burning in front of me so I can see my way toward improvement?"

"Something like that, Zach. Correct your mistakes and put them behind you. Blaming someone else for your shortcomings helps no one, especially you. You can't walk forward while you're looking behind you, so don't dwell on the past. Move ahead by improving yourself, correcting your mistakes as you go."

"Gosh, Mom, you always have something to say to straighten out my thinking." He smiled and gave me an affectionate pat on the shoulder as he headed for his basketball and the hoop outside.

26
Poster Girls

ey, Mom, are you mad at me for looking through the posters of girls in bathing suits when we were at the mall today? I saw you shake your head in disgust."

I had seen him looking through the posters, but I was disgusted with the proprietor for mixing in seductive pictures with the Garfield posters that children search through. "I wasn't shaking my head at you, Zach. I thought the adult oriented posters should have been located elsewhere." I really didn't like seeing females exploited in that way, but it was an issue Zach would have to address.

"I'm not so naive as to think that those types of pictures won't attract your attention, Zach. However, I was glad to see you thumb through them instead of gawking at each one.

The female bodies portrayed were beautiful and I knew teenagers were naturally curious. "I only caution you to satisfy your curiosity and not your lust when you look through such photos. Do not allow them to seduce you into believing that someone else's body is something that you must have, own, or crave, because it doesn't belong to you."

"I know, Mom. Do you really think that I would abuse a woman?"

"No, but some people do. Remember to appreciate and respect a thing of beauty and don't try to manipulate it or allow it to manipulate you."

"Mom, we've been discussing different kinds of pollution in school. Is there such a thing as mind pollution?"

I was glad to see him make the connection and agreed that pollution of the mind was important because it was so subtle. "Adopting an unhealthy point of view is a form of mind pollution and you must guard against it as vehemently as you protest against other forms of pollution."

"OK, Mom. Thanks for not getting angry."

27
Government Begins At Home

One advantage of having a child was the refresher course I received on grades K-12 that reminded me how many concepts had slipped my mind as a result of not being used.

"Hey, Mom," came a loud plea from the opposite end of the house, "will you help me with my school assignment?" Zach was studying leadership and adult responsibilities. "One question asks how parents know whether their child will be a responsible adult at age eighteen."

"History" I hailed from the kitchen.

"What history?" he shouted back.

Not wanting to continue the reverberating discussion in an echo chamber, I halted dinner preparation and joined him at the computer. "Your history." I began. "You started proving your level of responsibility to me when you were two." I reminded him how he had enjoyed riding his plastic "Bee" on the sidewalk in front of our house.

"Bee" was a 2 foot long yellow molded plastic riding toy in the shape of a giant bumble bee which originally had a noise maker attached to the wheels. This noisy feature had not bothered the general population for six months since his Aunt Sheryl had removed it one day after Zach rode it around her campsite at 6:00 a.m..

"I watched you from the front porch, but sometimes the phone interrupted and I had to leave for a moment and observe you through the window. I gave you specific instructions not to cross the two lines in the sidewalk which were about 50 feet apart. As I watched from inside, I saw you curl Bee under your legs, give a big push, and yell, 'wheeeeee Beeeeee' as you sped down the sidewalk toward the neighbor's driveway. Just as abruptly, you threw on the well worn "shoe" brakes and came to a halt inches inside the boundary line that I had established."

"I remember." Zach stated. "I loved that Bee."

"You certainly did. Later in the day, I observed you while you played with your friends." Unlike Zach, his friends rode their tricycles up and down the length of the neighborhood side walk, racing against him, and encouraging him to extend his boundaries when they thought I wasn't watching. "You always obeyed whatever boundaries I gave you, and as you proved your obedience for one boundary, I expanded your range. As you matured, I defined some limits for you and established appropriate consequences for your behavior. At other times, I allowed you to set the boundaries and observed your behavior."

"I know, Mom. You trusted me as long as I showed you I could make wise decisions."

"Right! By the time you are eighteen, you will have had sufficient practice making decisions, setting your own boundaries, and living within limits established for your protection. Your sense of responsibility has been developing gradually through the years. In order for government to be effective, it must begin at home at an early age. In this way you learn that a willingness to obey life's boundaries furnishes you with a sense of freedom, not shackles."

"Thanks, Mom. Hey, I'm hungry! What's for dinner?"

28

Breaking Up

ach came in from school a little more slowly than usual. He lacked the sparkle that often accompanied his arrival. His shoulders slumped a bit as he studied the floor. Although he said hello, it was automatic. Something was bothering him.

"Trouble today, Zach?" I asked.

He studied the floor further, then glanced up toward me. "I think I'm going to break up with my girl-friend, but I don't want to hurt her feelings. How can I tell her without making her mad?"

I was surprised and a bit puzzled. They had been good friends since second grade and had been very supportive of each other in school competitions for the past two years. "What's changed your feelings toward her? I remember the great respect you had for her all along. Is she the one who changed, or have you changed?"

"I'm not sure." he replied and then was silent for a while. "I just don't know how to tell her without making her mad at me."

I put my arm around him. "Maybe you're making it harder than it is. Be tactful in telling her the reasons you want to break up and take responsibility for the way you feel. Don't belittle her in any way; don't ignore her, and don't hesitate to support her kindly if she feels hurt by your decision. After all, it takes two to maintain a relationship, but only one to break it off." I explained to him that because she might not feel the same way he did, he should be as kind and courteous to her in the end of the relationship as he had been in the beginning.

He looked back at me with a wrinkled brow. "You mean I should be careful not to react to what she says or does?"

He had remembered our previous discussion about my divorce. "That's right! Act in accordance with your feelings, not hers, and do what you think is best. The right decision won't hurt anybody."

"Mom, when you told me about your divorce, it sounded like you were taking all the blame for things not going well. Do I have to assume the blame for breaking up?"

I shook my head and smiled. "No, Zach, I didn't assume the blame and you don't need to either, but we both need to take responsibility for the way we feel. Both your father and I made mistakes and we are each responsible for what we did and how we felt. Your girlfriend may have done something to hurt your feelings, perhaps without even knowing it, but you are the one feeling the hurt. She's still a worthwhile person even if you don't want to continue thinking of her as your girlfriend." I paused, then asked "Do you dislike her now?"

He shook his head somewhat impatiently. "No, I still like her. I just don't know how to be the kind of friend she wants me to be." There was a long silence and then, "I guess we need to talk before we decide to break up."

I nodded eagerly. "That would be good. Maybe your friendship is something that can be recycled instead of trashed."

He grinned. "That's a good idea, Mom. I'll tell her that." As he left for his paper route, I saw the old spring in his step again and he looked straight ahead as he walked.

29
Tides and Bulldozers

recall as a young adult how my mother often returned home from teaching first grade just in time to receive a phone call from our neighbor. Her role in the conversation was sometimes just to listen for 30 minutes. I tried never to interrupt her during this time because I understood that the phone call was her method of socializing in the evenings. I, too, enjoyed my time cradling the receiver between my chin and collar bone while preparing dinner and folding laundry since I also spent most evenings at home.

One evening I listened to the concerns of a friend while I was cutting twigs into two inch segments for Zach's castle project. He worked beside me on the kitchen stool and glued pieces together while I gently offered words of encouragement over the phone.

"Hey, Mom," Zach asked after I ended the phone conversation, "why did you spend so much time talking about the same subject to your friend? Wouldn't it have been faster to just tell her what you thought right off."

"Yes, you're right, but sometimes it's better to let ideas resemble the force of a gentle tide instead of a bulldozer."

"Huh? What do you mean by that?"

I reminded him about our trip to the ocean and some of the lessons we had learned there. We had spent many hours walking along the beach each day watching the actions of different tides. Some were gentle, rolling tides leaving sea shells intact. Others were dynamic, crashing tides, bulldozing their way toward shore, unloading pounds of crushed shells at our feet. Zach continued working at the castle, peeling dried glue from his fingers. "Remember how the tide rolled over the sandy beach and deposited its treasures on shore? Each overturning wave carved a pattern in the sand, clearing a place to deposit a sand dollar, shell, or piece of driftwood."

"Oh, yeah, I remember, we talked about how the wave kept working at it gradually."

"That's right, it's called perseverance, and it is as powerful as a bulldozer. My friend was upset about her situation and wasn't ready to look for a solution. If I had bull-dozed my opinion right off, she would have rejected my suggestions. Like the gentle tide, I had to prepare her thought to be receptive to a different idea before depositing a new one with her."

Zach positioned the last twig on the castle and began building the moat. "Darn it!" The rocks he was assembling along the moat fell into the gorge. "My hands just aren't steady enough to do this!"

"Don't get angry," I reassured him, "get good."

"You mean I should try to persevere?"

"Yes, anger is just an escape hatch. The only way you can learn from some situations is to stay with them. If you give up, you become your own enemy."

"What's so bad about giving up sometimes and just being average?" he argued. I looked at his tired eyes and I knew that he could learn very little in his current argumentative mood.

"Let's walk up to the malt shop while we think about that question?" I suggested.

Zach readily agreed and we discussed his favorite subjects such as changes in his basketball team's lineup as we made our way toward chocolate delights. On our return trip Zach asked why I had changed the topic earlier instead of answering his question about giving up. I paused before opening the gate to our yard and said, "Because you weren't really asking me a question, you were making a statement."

"Why do you say that?"

"Because words are outward symptoms expressing inward needs. Your words were telling me that you were tired and discouraged so that's what I responded to. Discouragement is a powerful self-destructive tool but it can be combated with gratitude. I just helped you to recede like the wave and find something that made you happy and for which you were grateful. Sometimes perseverance is a two cycle force. It's easier to push forward after you've taken a step back and expressed gratitude. Do you still feel tempted to give up on your castle project now?"

"No, Mom, I'm ready to finish it. What do you know about bridges?"

30
Ego is Your Goliath

My book report is about..." I heard Zach recite in front of the bathroom mirror as I passed by the door. "What are you doing?" I questioned. "I'm practicing my oral book report for tomorrow. I wish I didn't have to present it to the entire class. I hate speaking in front of large groups."

Zach's attitude was not foreign to me. I could well remember moments in public speaking class when perspiration soaked my blouse as I tried to calm a shaky voice and trembling gestures. Even smiling was a chore on such occasions. I tried to recall how I managed to survive the torture.

"What makes you so nervous about speaking in front of people?" I inquired.

"I don't like people looking at me and waiting for me to make a mistake." He replied.

"Are the other kids in your class scared too?"

"Not all of them. Some of them have such giant egos that nothing could phase them."

Giant, I thought. This is a Goliath problem. "You're running away from your Goliath." I stated in an attempt to start him thinking. "How?" he asked.

"You mentioned giant egos," I began. "Both you with your awkward shyness and your popular self-confident classmates have ego problems - Goliaths that need to be defeated."

Zach gave me a puzzled look and asked, "In what way?"

"Both of you are acting self-centered by being concerned with what the world thinks of you. You are awaiting the approval of others in order to be happy. You need to get 'Zach' out of the way so you can focus on the real issues. Your shyness is not meekness, because meekness carries with it the power of obedience. Be obedient to your true fearless nature and run toward the Goliath problem and defeat it."

Zach approached me slowly and sat down. "How do I get myself out of the way?" came his inquiry.

"You must change your self-conscious image," I replied. "Instead of worrying about what people might think of you during your book report, concern yourself with how you might help them enjoy learning something new. Your assignment is really to teach the class something about the book you read. Find a way to make it enjoyable for them to learn the information. The words that come from your mouth may be important, but the joy that shines through you in your delivery of the information will make it special.

"Are you sure I still won't blush, shake, and squeak while I'm doing that?"

"I'm sure," I replied. "Remove the attention from you and focus it on helping someone else to have a good time. At the end of the occasion you'll discover that your joy is found in the good you do for others. When good is made obvious, people tend not to notice minor flaws."

"But what if they don't like my report?" he pleaded.

"Be a salesman and display your genuine interest and kindness. Set the mood in the class before you give your report. Be considerate when you are listening to the reports given by others and only make supportive remarks about them. If you discover a weakness in someone else and help that person overcome it instead of pointing it out, you will be rewarded with a new friend. Hide a person's faults; don't announce them to others. Treat them the way you would like to be treated."

Zach stood up and walked back into the bathroom. "Now, what are you doing?" I posed.

"I'm going to rework my book report and add a few laughs."

31
Step Ahead

ach arrived from school looking irritable and attempted a brief explanation of his day.

"Hey, Mom, I just want to warn you that I had a horrible day! I'm going to my room to listen to music."

I appreciated the warning, but decided to disagree with his solution. "It sounds like you need to sit on the step, instead of listening to music." As a young child, whenever Zach was out of sorts, he would pick a step on the stairway upstairs where he thought he could change his mood and see things from a happier perspective. He selected a different step each time, depending on the gravity of the situation. Higher steps seemed to be reserved for more complicated problems. Quickly, though, he would return from the stairway with a smile on his face and an apology for his misbehavior or poor attitude.

"I know, Mom, but my problems are bigger now. Our stairway may not have enough steps."

"You can still step ahead." I assured him. "You are in control of your emotions and you are the only person who can change the expression on your face and your mood."

"But, Mom" he pleaded.

"You can do it if you try." I was insistent because I thought he was giving up much too easily. He needed a station identification break. "Look around and see something that delights you. See the world through the eyes of something else if you don't like what your eyes see.

I pointed to the cat who had been sneaking around the table, waiting for Zach to turn his back so she could perch on his chair and swipe his snack while he was obsessed with his depression. "Look at the pup" I suggested. "She's been tearing around the house testing my patience and waiting for me to acknowledge her presence with a firm warning about house speed limits. Or look outside at the squirrels breakdancing on the lawn, bragging how they once again managed to get past my anti-squirrel guards on the bird feeder and upend the entire unit.

Slowly a smile started to come across his

face. It was hard not to laugh at such animal antics. "You can change your mood faster than I can say Jiminy Cricket. Practice this technique and you will never need to rely on pills, people, situations, or music to alter your moods. You will be able to enjoy the happiness that is readily available to you. Your joy is an effortless expression because it's your natural state."

"You mean it's not something I have to work at?"

"No, Zach, you just have to accept its benefits."

"Where's my camera, Mom? I want to take a picture of that crazy, break-dancing squirrel."

"It's on the stairway to your room." I pointed to his thinking step and smiled.

32
Education Is Appreciation

I often wonder what Zach's occupation will be when he grows up. When he was little, he frequently could be heard in the hall closet saying, "Going up, please" as he pretended to usher people in and out of an elevator. His elementary years had him dreaming of being a dolphin trainer and he requested a life-sized dolphin for his bathtub. More recently, though, he has been attracted to the idea of being a banker like his Uncle Steve. This attraction to banking is in part due to the number of fringe benefits he sees his Uncle enjoy, such as free tickets to professional sporting events. The other side of it is that he adores his Uncle and would like to please him. Whatever Zach's decision in the future I hope he finds as much joy in his job as he has in his imaginary occupations.

"Hey, Mom, in school this week we are doing pretend job interviews." He explained that in order to interview for some jobs, a college education was required. "Some of the factory jobs pay well and don't require much education. If I can make enough money working in a local factory, do I need to go to college?"

I knew college wasn't the right learning environment for everyone. I had known some students who graduated from college without learning as much as those who eagerly greeted learning opportunities in their daily lives. A college education offers a variety of learning experiences, exposing students to diverse cultures, opinions, and problem solving techniques, but ultimately, the student is responsible for providing a mind conducive to learning; one that is receptive to new ideas and discussions. I explained that the purpose of education was to improve a person's quality of life and had nothing to do with money; it had to do with appreciation.

"Education teaches you to appreciate your environment, whatever it may be." I reminded him how he viewed photographs before he started taking his own photos. He thumbed through photos very quickly looking at them only to recall events or identify friends. Until he stood behind the camera lens and shot his own pictures, developed them, enlarged and printed them, he didn't fully appreciate the skills involved in true photography.

"Actually performing the necessary photographic techniques taught you an appreciation for your surroundings that you hadn't previously experienced."

"I know what you mean. Now I automatically frame what I see as though I were always taking pictures. I consider lighting, focus, depth of field, and shutter speed."

"Precisely, and as a result of your learning something new, you can better appreciate the time and effort spent by others when you view their photos. The clearer you understand an issue or object, the more fully you appreciate its purpose." I continued to explain to Zach that the real product of education is a person's character, and without character development, civilization is merely training people." Zach pondered my remark briefly and then asked why it was so important.

"Because we develop in ourselves a stationary intellectual inertia when we refuse to think for ourselves and vacate our own ambitions and sense of what is right. World peace is not a goal for society; it is a by-product of the Golden Rule. Education develops your character, expanding your thinking, teaching you through history the wisdom of treating others the way in which you would like to be treated."

"Do you want me to go to college?"

"I would like for you to, but that will be your decision when you're eighteen. Whatever path you select, work to improve your quality of life by gaining a fuller appreciation of the world around you."

"Hey, Mom, how about a game of chess? I learned a new move that I think you'll really appreciate!"

33
Mealtime Humor

My parents and siblings had well developed senses of humor. It's astonishing that we all didn't suffer from digestive problems as a consequence of our extended stretch of laughter at the dinner table. I could introduce a solemn topic of conversation, and almost before I completed my thought, each family member contributed a pun or play on words that brought an abrupt end to any serious discussion. Zach also inherited this amusing trait and found numerous opportunities to shake me silly with his hysterics. Keeping up with his sharp humor was a challenge for me especially since he could remember every joke he had ever heard and I had difficulty remembering punch lines.

"Hey, Mom, why are your dinner portions so small this evening?"

"I'm on a diet, and I'd like your help with it this time. I've gained way too much weight recently."

"Ah, Mom, you've only gained weight in three places - the delicatessen, the bakery, and the pizza parlor."

"You mean I've been on a seafood diet - only eating what I can see?"

"Yeah, Mom, maybe you should switch diets and try to be a light eater."

"Oh, so now I can only eat when there is a light on?"

"Don't get discouraged, Mom. Just think of all the people you are helping by not dieting."

"Who would that be, Zach?"

"All the people in Kansas and Nebraska. If you went on a diet, they'd probably have a grain surplus and that could cause them economic distress."

"Maybe I should just take up sky-diving and forget to pull the ripcord."

"Don't do that, Mom. If you jumped from a plane, someone might mistake you for a total eclipse of the sun!"

34

Save the Garden and the Song

treasure my flower gardens. They bring me such joy by reminding me of the lessons I've learned there. On one occasion while I was mixing mulch, sand, and peat moss into my compost pile Zach asked, "Hey, Mom, what does it mean to win the battle but lose the war?" He had heard the comment on TV in a political debate.

"It means people spend their energy on small problems and miss the total effect. They need to view situations from a broader perspective and select their actions more carefully. They need to do something that will change the total outcome."

"I don't understand, what do you mean?"

I stopped shoveling the compost and looked around the yard. "Consider the garden." I said. "There are many chemicals on the market that could fertilize the soil and act as pesticides. They are easy to apply, but very expensive for our budget and harmful to our environment." Zach was running his hand through the bucket of sand watching it sift through his fingers. "If I use pesticides and herbicides I will effectively control the bugs and weeds and win the garden battle, but I will lose the birds and frogs who are attracted to the bugs and thus lose the war because my garden will have no song."

"Then what is the solution if you can't use chemicals?"

"Compost" I said pointing to the large bin.

"Why compost?" he questioned.

"Our compost is a mixture of food scraps, yard clippings, soil, mulch, sand and peat moss which I mix with the soil around the flowers to nourish the garden. The compost fertilizes the soil and helps the plants grow to maturity. A mature garden seldom has weed problems so there's no need to use a herbicide. The decomposing matter attracts bugs and slugs which attract frogs and birds. The frogs eat the slugs and thereby protect my hostas and the birds eat insects and drop wild flower seeds into the garden on their way to the birdbath. Caterpillars attach their larvae to the wild milkweed planted by the birds and become butterflies to adorn the garden in later months. With only a little intervention from me, my garden can be a perpetual joy without using chemicals."

Zach looked up toward the tree branches overhead and listened to the various song-birds. At night he had enjoyed listening to the night sounds produced by the crickets, frogs, and locusts. "I understand." he said. "You're looking at the whole picture - every-thing that lives in the garden, not just the flowers."

"That's right." I added. "By considering all aspects and choosing to use a natural compost instead of a chemical which han-dles only one problem, I can win the garden war by saving the garden and the song."

35
Vice Money

n recent years Zach and I spent twenty minutes each day in the spa discussing current events. Our conversations were usually humorous and probably entertained the neighbors since our raised voices undoubtedly carried over the roar of the bubbling jets. On one occasion I decided to turn the tables on Zach and asked, "Hey, Zach, why do kids nowadays smoke, drink, and use drugs?"

"For the same lame reason they did when you were a kid!" he laughed.

"What reason is that?" I asked.

"They want to feel grown up and in charge of their lives."

Zach was only fourteen, but I had seen some of his school mates smoking as they rode their bikes around town. There was also a rumor that drugs were available near the Middle School, so I asked him to talk about his feelings on this issue.

"To me, it's very simple." he stated firmly. "I don't feel the need to use them."

"Why is that?" I asked. "What makes you

so different from your school mates who do smoke?"

"You do!" came his quick reply. "You have always treated me as an adult and have allowed me the freedom to make many decisions for myself. I don't need to pretend that I'm a grown up, because you make me feel like one."

His answer startled me because I had prepared myself for a more typical response.

"What about you, Mom, why didn't you use drugs?"

"I was usually happy" I replied "and if I wasn't, then I just changed my view point to something more pleasant. My thoughts improved my attitude much more quickly than could any drug and thoughts were always available. Besides," I continued, "I probably wasn't patient enough to take the time to learn how to like the smell and taste of cigarettes and alcohol. I find their odor to be quite offensive."

"I do too, Mom." Zach agreed. "I sure enjoy this spa!"

"I do too, Zach. I'm glad I had enough vice money to pay for it."

"What is vice money, Mom?"

"It's the money I spend on items which lift my spirits, such as flowers and vacations. I calculated once how much it would cost me monthly to purchase cigarettes and alcohol if I used them. It was quite a large sum, so I decided to put that amount of money into a special savings account and use it to buy items that pleased me. I don't like smoking or drinking, but I do enjoy other pleasures, so I call it my vice account."

"That's great!" he exclaimed. "I heard on TV recently that the price of cigarettes is going to dramatically increase soon. If it does, maybe your vice account can finance that digital camera for the computer!"

36
Right Relationships

"Go baseline! Jam! Turn-around..pump fake... power up! That's it! Follow your shot! Good job!" I was giving Zach instructions for his offensive and defensive moves in basketball. "Block out! Rebound...outlet pass! Now, hustle down the court. Meet your pass! Fake left; jump shot! Nice basket! Whew, I'm tired." I turned to leave the court and go inside the house.

"Hey, Mom, before you go inside can we practice free-throws and talk a bit?"

I located my hand towel and water bottle. "I guess I still have enough energy for that. What's up?"

Zach addressed the free-throw line and began his first set of ten attempts. Strip! went the first shot. He missed the next three attempts, but instead of getting frustrated he closed his eyes very briefly and then opened them and let fly a successful shot. "Very good!" I complimented him. "You restored your proper form."

"Yeah, I remembered to check my gauges this time."

I had instructed him at a younger age not to think about what was wrong with a missed shot, but to imagine the perfect shot and focus on how to perform it correctly with his elbow up, facing the basket, arm extended upward, wrist flexed, and fingers extended with the middle finger pointing the way. "Good follow through!" I remarked as he practiced the correct form again.

"You know, Mom, I was just remembering what you told me about my father being a pilot. You said he gathered as much information as possible from various sources during a flight, but sometimes he had to rely only on the gauges of his instrument panel when he flew in conditions where he couldn't see."

"That's right. Sometimes he had to trust what his eyes couldn't tell him about the sky and the ground."

"Yeah, well, I think the same idea applies to other situations also."

"In what way?"

Zach continued practicing his free-throws

and I rebounded for him." Well, a good relationship with a girl includes proper form, too, for proper behavior. Sometimes when I'm upset I find it easier to get along with a person if I take the time to close my eyes, check my gauges the way I do in basketball, and just remember what I feel."

Zach's comment showed me that he was responding to his respect for his friend instead of being lured by temptation. "That's good, in that way you are setting yourself up to succeed. Feelings of love can't rule when you rule."

"Do you think I'm ignoring the problem by doing that?"

"No," I replied, "you are separating the problem from the person. They are not the same. You can continue to be supportive and feel affection for a person while disarming a problem." I reminded Zach of the lighthouses we had visited on Nantucket Island and how the storm raged all around them but they never became part of the storm. They remained a beacon of light guiding ships to safety. "You are resembling the lighthouse when you refuse to get caught up in a problem, keeping your focus on what's right."

Zach seemed pleased with the direction of our conversation and we discussed the jealousy that some of his friends felt in their relationships. I explained that jealousy is like a bad wind that blows out the lamp of reason and can prevent a person from enjoying a relationship. "If you check the gauge you've been taught to live by, just as you check the form you've been taught to shoot by before you act, you will have fewer problems to correct later and you won't put yourself in a situation which encourages mistakes."

"That's pretty hard for some people to understand, Mom." Zach related an incident he had experienced with one of his friends who was jealous of his girlfriend's association with other guys.

"What finally happened with them?" I asked.

Zach made his last shot and started spinning the ball on his finger. "They broke up. The guy let his jealousy get to him. He complained to his girlfriend so much about the other guys that she decided to date one of them instead of him."

I gave an understanding nod and explained that sometimes what people expect is what they get, so they should learn to guard their thoughts carefully. "Thoughts of jealousy always prove to be destructive because they cloud thinking."

Zach placed the ball on the court and sat down on it. "Mom," he asked in a very serious tone, "what is love and how can I recognize it in my own relationships?"

I looked around me, but I could find nothing to use as an example. "Examine the effects of your feelings." I proposed. "If your feelings and actions tend to liberate a person, making them feel fearless; and if you patiently support them; and if your qualities harmonize and blend creatively with theirs; and if your feelings flow continuously toward them, then what you feel is love and it will satisfy your needs." Zach offered an understanding nod and I asked, "By the way, how's your girlfriend?"

"She's not my girlfriend, Mom."

"Why not? You like her don't you?"

"Sure, but she's dating another guy."

"Does that upset you?"

Zach passed me the ball. "No, it doesn't

bother me. She goes through boyfriends so quickly that I'd much rather be her friend on a long-term basis."

37

Measuring Up

My pre-parenting years were filled with thoughts of myself, largely. I did what I wanted, when I wanted, and with whom I wanted. I observed those situations in life which intrigued me and didn't give much thought to others. That hasn't been the case for the past 15 years.

Zach has forced me to experience life, not only with him, but through the eyes of others. In his early years I had to learn to think like a frog, dog, duck, pig, turtle and dinosaur in order to participate in his molded plastic make-believe world on the floor of the living room. I had to consider the thoughts and actions of other children his age, not my own, when filling the role of adversary in fictional wargames when no playmates were available that day. I learned to focus as intensely as a child on the faces of cards in a memory game so that I would be a challenge in the competition and not a sorry disappointment. As his motor skills began to develop and Zach became interested in swimming, riding a bike, and throwing frisbees, footballs, and baseballs, it was necessary for me to devise ways of explaining balance, center of gravity, torque, levers, Bernoulli's principle of aerodynamics, and Archimedes' principle of buoyancy in terms that a young child could understand.

In his elementary years it was my job to provide Zach with answers for why the sky was blue, why an arm submerged in water appeared to be bent, and why hummingbirds chose not to sing. Some of his questions I had never considered previously and I struggled to keep pace with his curiosity, knowing that the questions would only get harder. I had been a strong academic student in school, but this was a more demanding test than any I had ever taken. I realized that the best way for me to prepare for his future questions was to become as perceptive as he in my daily life. I began questioning everything, even why my garden attracted certain insects. Interestingly, I found not only the answers to my questions, but answers to problems in life.

One day when I had been particularly pensive Zach asked if I were searching for myself. He had heard that phrase used by a school counselor in a presentation on adolescence. I replied that I didn't need to look for myself because I knew exactly where I was; in the middle of the picture. I was looking for the outer limits of the frame. He gave my response some careful thought and then suggested that my picture might really be an infinite mural in which case I might never find the frame.

With frequent perceptive comments such as this it was no surprise to me that Zach didn't seem to face those problems that psychologists suggest children experience in their development. Zach considered negative attributes to be counterfeits; deceiving and defrauding people, with no true value. His aim was to express their counterparts; resembling the positive. He wasn't jealous because he was grateful. He wasn't bitter because he was affectionate. He wasn't irrational because he was discerning. He wasn't depressed because he was buoyant. He didn't struggle with being a male because he learned to be a man from the start; a man with both masculine and feminine qualities:

strong, loyal, and courageous in a patient, gentle, and loving manner. He didn't worry about how to convince a girl or anyone else to like him; he just demonstrated those qualities he wanted to attract in others. He proved himself by meeting the daily challenges to what he believed.

I was pleased, but not surprised, when one day a school official contacted me and relayed an incident she had witnessed during lunch at the middle school. A group of boys taunted Zach as he sat at the lunch table with his friends. They stood over him and called him names, challenging him to a fight. He made no comment until one remark defamed his friend. At that point Zach rose from his chair and placed his hands on his hips. At 6'1" he stood several inches above his opponent and the onlookers anticipated a fight. Zach looked down at his rival and laughed quietly. "That," he said shaking his head, "is so untrue that it is funny. You really have a great sense of humor." This was not at all what his adversary had expected and, not knowing how to respond, the antagonist departed with his followers. "How does he do that?" asked the school official. "He's strong enough to defend himself against most people and yet he won't even offend his enemies!" I agreed with her assessment and said, "That's just Zach. He'd rather make them his friends."

38

Advancing Years

Because we often judge people by their age, not by their wisdom, and are therefore self-deceived, we impose this same fallacious standard upon our children throughout their advancing years. We consider them too young for some pleasures and too old for others and we chide them when we think they are not "acting their age." If we allow time to be our teacher, it will take a toll on us.

Our family made it a point never to discuss age. My friends were amazed that I had no notion of my parents' ages other than knowing they served our country as young adults during World War II. I was taught from the start that cultivating a newness of understanding was more important than counting years. I desperately tried to absorb my father's wisdom before I reached adulthood, thinking that some day we would be mental equals. I am now middle-aged and realize that I still have a long way to go. Old ideas represented a conservative approach to life, whereas, newness offered a stimulant for growth. Age and growth were not considered interactive. One did not produce the other.

When Zach reached his teenage years and I noticed him struggling at times with changes in his stature, voice, and physical appearance I decided it was time for an "oil job." He had commented that with his changing voice he didn't like to sing because he never knew from note to note whether he would be a soprano or a baritone. The absence of his singing produced a noticeable change in the household since I had become accustomed to his humming a pop tune as he wandered from room to room. I also had noticed him blushing and retreating whenever his female friends passed by the house. He began disparaging himself, thinking he had very little to offer other people his age.

"Zach," I said one day after listening to his complaints, "you've gotten squeaky; you need an oil job!" Instantly I received a what-have-I-done-now look along with a slight grunt. "You're accepting this teenage scenario of displeasure with your life and you're using age as an excuse. Instead of focusing on your inabilities at this point in your life and complaining, find the "oil" - what is right with you - and stop the squeak."

"I've tried, Mom, but the oil doesn't last long. It runs right off."

"Maybe it's because you have not prepared your surface to receive it."

"What?" He cocked his head inquisitively.

"I mean that gratitude is necessary to clean away the negative thoughts to make room for the positive ones. Without gratitude, your oil runs right over the dirt and grime and never lubricates anything useful. When you're grateful for what you have, life becomes smoother, a lot easier, and fewer faults appear to your view. Lubricate your thoughts and get them working for you, don't let them sludge up with discouragement."

I could tell that Zach understood my point, but he was struggling with accepting it.

"But, Mom, I feel so tall, heavy, and slow. What do I do with these feelings?"

"We have enough demolition experts in

this world, Zach; what we need are more builders. We are plagued with critics, paparazzi, and people looking only for cata-strophes and the bad in what we do. Be a magnet and attract good things in your life. Your height is beneficial in basketball, and you are just the right speed for enjoying the world as you pass by. As for your weight, take time to enjoy the seasoning and appearance of food before you eat it. Satisfy your hunger instead of your appetite. If you are busy counting your blessings there will be no time to count calories. As in every thing else, you must change your thoughts before you can change your body. You have many good qualities that you can look to for satisfac-tion. You don't need to be impressed with a good physique. An important aspect of physical fitness is that your body must be able to accomplish whatever you demand of it. Fitness isn't simply a measure of weight and girth, it begins with being mentally fit - exercising the right ideas."

"Are you saying it's OK for me to be heavy?"

"No, Zach, fitness is important. I'm saying that you must adopt a healthy attitude before you can expect a healthy body. Diets, pills, and special foods are only a temporary solution to part of the problem. You must consider the broader picture - your entire well-being - and make your adjustments accordingly."

"I know" he said "so that I'll be sure to win the war and not just one battle."

"Right. You have all you need to be successful in life. Keep your mind clear, transparent, and let goodness shine through you."

"I want to be successful, Mom, but I may come across lots of problems in the future and I'm not sure how to avoid all of them."

"There's really only one problem, Zach: being able to distinguish the difference between right and wrong. You know what right motive is. Each time you choose the right action, your future choices become clearer and easier to make."

"Maybe I'll just stay here and raise my family near you when I grow up."

"I always want us to be close, Zach, but you need to test the waters for yourself. A teacher told me once that a ship in the harbor is safe, but that's not what ships were built for. You must live what you know and not be content to just sit around knowing it. Living teaches you how to pass your light of wisdom on to others." I reminded Zach of a song we had sung in earlier years about "One Little Candle" and how it signified that the beauty of a candle is that it can light a thousand others. "As you grow in grace - in loving, forgiving, being merciful and just, poised and fearless in your joy - you will find that the opposite attributes have less effect on you. You will be, in your living, your own recommendation for everything that is good." Zach remained very pensive. When he was a young child we prepared for vacations by packing our own bags. I had him check the contents of his suitcase before we left to be sure that he hadn't packed any negative thoughts or problems. This enabled us to begin each journey on a positive note and maintain the joy throughout the trip since neither of us would willingly admit to having packed any troubles for vacation. "Pack your bags carefully, Zach, and hitch your wagon to a star as Emerson suggested."

Zach appeared satisfied with our discussion and commented, "Mom, these long stories that you've spent so much time telling me through the years have made the lessons easy to remember and I like them. Did you ever just want to give me an abridged version sometimes?"

I gazed into his sparkling blue-green eyes and embraced both of his shoulders. These long stories had taken a lot of time and effort when we were rushed, but I believed they were important so I hadn't abridged them, but delivered them with unhurried peace. "These long stories are your Ark, Zach, a haven during the storms of your life. The concepts that I've shared with you over the years and the lessons you've learned and implemented in your life are for your continued preservation when I'm no longer at your side. I have given you an ark of protection for all time, but only you can decide to come in out of the rain."

39
Remember When

Hey, Mom, remember when we used to tell each other stories and talk before bedtime? And how you and Granddad would tell me about Hiawatha's adventures? Hiawatha always seemed to have the same problems that I had. Remember when every bedtime ended with singing Over the Rainbow? Can we do that again?"

"Sure, Zach, we can do that. Do you want to do that instead of playing our guitars together before bedtime?"

"Gosh, no, Mom. I want to do it all. Maybe we should start earlier, like right after supper!"

"Sounds good to me, Zach."

"Hey, Mom, remember when I was four and you were real young, when you had long hair that tickled my face?

"Remember how I would curl up next to you on the front porch glider and we would listen to the night sounds and watch the sunlight disappear behind the trees while we talked about the old days when my pajamas had feet in them?

"Remember when Grandma had warm cookies on her table just waiting for me to arrive from school, and an hour or so of free time to listen to my stories before Granddad would read to me about Where the Wild Things Are?

"Remember when we sat on the front porch and watched the storms come in and I would curl close to you so you could run your fingers through my hair and we'd talk about shadows?

"Remember when we'd suck juice from oranges to get the peanut butter off the roofs of our mouths, and race the bath water out of the tub?

"Remember when I was older and you taught me how to ride my bike? First I learned with training wheels and then you took them off and ran along beside me while you pushed me all around the stadium track...for miles. You stayed with me and when I fell off, your kisses even made my bruises feel better.

"Remember when we played basketball with Uncle Steve, football with Justin, and baseball with the neighborhood kids under the street light?

"Remember when we sang songs with Aunt Sheryl and played card games with Grandma and Granddad and everybody was happy?

"Remember when I started school and I was worried about finding new friends and you told me I would find them by being the kind of person I wanted to have as a friend?

"Remember when Grandma and Granddad would pick me up from school on rainy days and ask me how my day went and I usually said that it was good? And if it wasn't, you would always help me find the joy and the lesson in what had happened?"

"Yes, Binker, I remember those times."

"I think about those times now whenever I'm away from you so I don't feel lonely."

∞

Indeed, I remember those times well. I recall how his spine stuck out as he curled up next to me on the glider, and the sweet fragrance of baby shampoo that was released with every stroke of my fingers through his thick golden hair.

I remember the sense of calm brought on by our discussions during the storms, and how we watched the last few rays of sunlight disappear through the filtering leaves of the sugar maples across the street as the mourning doves cooed the approaching summer rain.

I remember the old bathtub trick that my mother had used with me to get me out of the tub before the filmy soap ring stuck to my body and how well it worked with Zach too.

I remember the evenings spent rubbing his sturdy growing legs because my mother had rubbed mine and understood well how tired they were after the long hard days of playing dual roles in war, cowboys and indians, super-heroes, and sports stars.

I remember warm embraces that turned his mournful eyes into sparkling smiles the way my father's loving arms calmed me and set my world aright.

I remember it all.

40
What is a Parent?

My single friends have frequently grilled me on what it is like to be a parent. I have contemplated the answer ever since.

A parent is one who hides after jumping out of the shower in order to snatch a few moments alone before someone notices the water is no longer running.

A parent is one who can maintain a degree of sanity while enduring children in the home who are practicing to become demolition experts.

A parent is one who has developed an iron stomach and awkward smile from eating the special Parent Day concoctions prepared by an enthusiastic and creative youngster.

A parent is one who enjoys scraping melted crayons out of the heat register after noticing that the house smells like a candle factory.

A parent is one who is relieved to hear a child practice Pop Goes the Weasel on the piano because it gives the mind something new to hear in its sleep after two weeks of

Yankee Doodle.

A parent is one who manages to hide the distressed, nauseous feeling from repairing bloody appendages after being summoned home from work by an anxious phone call.

A parent is one who cringes when Grandma buys the child a drum set and turns the nervous energy of the little hands into nervous racket for all the neighbors to notice.

A parent is one who believes that fixing a five course meal is no longer an attempt to feed the multitudes, but rather a sustained effort to prepare and serve food which no one will eat.

A parent is one who spends hours after midnight typing a report for work only to realize much too late that everything has been spelled phonetically.

EPILOGUE

One evening some friends and I were gathered around the dining room table playing Rummicube while our sons were huddled around the computer chatting with friends in cyberspace. We were sharing humorous tales about raising children when one of them asked me which parent/child lecture session had been the most difficult for me.

Zach and I had openly discussed concerns from a very early age and no topic seemed too insurmountable to broach. I reflected on some of the topics Zach and I had discussed and couldn't conclude that one was any more difficult than another. Each lesson I taught him I felt was an important one. It had to be consistent with each previous lesson and founded on the same principles established when he was born. I couldn't alter my approach to life in midstream. If what I believed about ever-present good were true, then it could be demonstrated in every situation. Since the basis for each discussion was always the same, only the method of communicating the idea changed. The only difficulty in presenting any of the issues was in making the good choice as attractive as the bad.

Being a parent is seldom an easy job, but it can be rewarding for both parent and child. From the beginning, I tried to raise Zach to be a responsible adult. I had to be careful not to create in him, at an early age, needs that might later lead to behaviors or use of substances harmful to him.

I heard a holocaust survivor once explain how giving up was a permanent solution to a temporary problem. This powerful statement made me question why I had chosen life during my darkest hour. After considering some of the problems I had faced, I realized the lessons from my childhood had been the reason for my perseverance. In teaching me their way of life when I was young, my parents had given me the solutions to my future problems. Like my parents, I couldn't possibly anticipate all of the challenges my child might encounter some day, but I could provide him with this same Ark of Protection by teaching him values now which would later provide answers to his questions. In this way, I was preparing him to successfully meet challenges by supplying him with the solutions in advance. The right path wouldn't be something for which he'd have to search in desperation, it would be revealed to him in a new light when he needed it most.

Helping to guide Zach through his youth also acted as a refresher course for me, reminding me that the truths I was imparting to him were equally applicable to me in an adult world. Certain qualities should never be outgrown. One is never too old to be observant, patient, trustworthy, kind, compassionate, or sincere. The Golden Rule should never tarnish or become antiquated. Love really is more powerful than hate, and every seed of ethics planted in childhood can be harvested throughout life. These rules for life were for both of us, and Zach was quick to remind me whenever I failed to demonstrate the principles I taught. The birth of Zachary was a rebirth for me and a blessing that continues to unfold.

Now Zach is fifteen and he's as kind and sensitive as he was at two. We're still buddies, we talk and play and have lots of fun. I don't get down on my hands and knees anymore, but I try to hold my own against him on the basketball court. I don't look for his good qualities to change much in the future. I may be wrong, but I don't think so.

My hope for Zach is that he will keep his joy.

Measurement
by Harold Spicer
(my father)

"How big is a soul?" she asked of me,
small brown eyes wide, pleadingly.
"As big as a house? As high as a star?"

"Only as big as you feel you are," I said.
What more was there to say,
When Infinity lies in the grasp of the
Hand
And Eternity is ever Today?

(used with permission of the author)

About the Author

Sylvia Spicer (M.A. in Education with an emphasis in sport biomechanics) is an experienced secondary school and collegiate teacher and coach. Since the age of 14 her occupations have been as varied as her interests. She was an accomplished 7-sport varsity athlete in high school and college, a Big Ten coach, a corporate manager, a family service caseworker, a fraud investigator, a camp counselor, a nurse's aid, and a care provider for the terminally ill.

As a single parent she has experienced the joys and despair of doing minor electrical, plumbing and appliance repairs; landscaping for beauty and flood control; major carpentry projects e.g., constructing a 2-story fort, garden buildings, a loft in her son's bedroom, and hardwood flooring in the house. She supported her son's interests by creating quilts from his favorite outgrown clothes; decorating costumes and birthday cakes in the likeness of his favorite super-heroes; constructing mountain landscapes for his train; molding paper mache action figures, making wooden cars, trucks, whistles, and musical instruments; teaching him to fish, camp, acquire sport skills; making up bedtime stories and songs that included him and his friends; using recycled magazines to make personalized comic books; and baking his favorite cookies for after school treats. Between chauffeur trips to school activities, athletic practices, and sporting events, she enjoyed woodworking, gardening, writing songs and poetry, studying whales, and volunteering her time at the public library and humane society. All required the creative management of her time and resources and provided her with challenges which required her to rely heavily on values she had been taught as a child. Now, in retrospect, she completes the circle and reveals the elucidating episodes of her adult life through the lessons she taught her son from the moment he awoke and first uttered the words "Hey, Mom" until his fifteenth year.